Maximize Your
ROUTER SKILLS
with Ken Burton

POPULAR WOODWORKING BOOKS
CINCINNATI, OHIO
www.popularwoodworking.com

READ THIS IMPORTANT SAFETY NOTICE

To prevent accidents, keep safety in mind while you work. Use the safety guards installed on power equipment; they are for your protection. When working on power equipment, keep fingers away from saw blades, wear safety goggles to prevent injuries from flying wood chips and sawdust, wear hearing protection and consider installing a dust vacuum to reduce the amount of airborne sawdust in your woodshop. Don't wear loose clothing, such as neckties or shirts with loose sleeves, or jewelry, such as rings, necklaces or bracelets, when working on power equipment. Tie back long hair to prevent it from getting caught in your equipment. People who are sensitive to certain chemicals should check the chemical content of any product before using it. The authors and editors who compiled this book have tried to make the contents as accurate and correct as possible. Plans, illustrations, photographs and text have been carefully checked. All instructions, plans and projects should be carefully read, studied and understood before beginning construction. Due to the variability of local conditions, construction materials, skill levels, etc., neither the author nor Popular Woodworking Books assumes any responsibility for any accidents, injuries, damages or other losses incurred resulting from the material presented in this book. Prices listed for supplies and equipment were current at the time of publication and are subject to change.

METRIC CONVERSION CHART

to convert	to	multiply by
Inches	Centimeters	2.54
Centimeters	Inches	0.4
Feet	Centimeters	30.5
Centimeters	Feet	0.03
Yards	Meters	0.9
Meters	Yards	1.1

Distributed in Canada by Fraser Direct
100 Armstrong Avenue
Georgetown, Ontario L7G 5S4
Canada

Distributed in the U.K. and Europe by David & Charles
Brunel House
Newton Abbot
Devon TQ12 4PU
England
Tel: (+44) 1626 323200
Fax: (+44) 1626 323319
E-mail: postmaster@davidandcharles.co.uk

Distributed in Australia by Capricorn Link
P.O. Box 704
Windsor, NSW 2756
Australia

Visit our Web site at www.popularwoodworking.com for information on more resources for woodworkers.

Other fine Popular Woodworking Books are available from your local bookstore or direct from the publisher.

11   10   09   08   07   5   4   3   2   1

Library of Congress Cataloging-in-Publication Data

Burton, Kenneth S.
  Maximize your router skills / with Ken Burton.
     p. cm.
ISBN 10: 1-55870-779-4 (pbk. : alk. paper)
ISBN 13: 978-1-55870-779-5 (pbk. : alk. paper)
  1. Routers (Tools) 2. Woodwork. I. Title.
  TT203.5.B97 2007
  684'.083--dc22
                              2007009930

Acquisitions editor: David Thiel
Senior editor: Jim Stack
Designer: Brian Roeth
Production coordinator: Mark Griffin
Photographer: Ken Burton
Photographer chapter openers: Donna H. Chiarelli
Illustrator: Jim Stack

F+W PUBLICATIONS, INC.

DEDICATION *For Susan, Sarah and Emma — you're the best!*

ABOUT THE AUTHOR

Ken Burton has been working with wood professionally for the past 25 years. He holds a Bachelor of Science degree in Industrial Arts education from Millersville University of Pennsylvania and a Master of Fine Arts degree in Woodworking and Furniture Design from the School for American Crafts at the Rochester Institute of Technology.

Currently, Burton operates Windy Ridge Woodworks in New Tripoli, Pennsylvania where he designs and builds original furniture, custom cabinetry and interiors. During the summer, he teaches woodworking workshops at the Yestermorrow Design/Build School in Warren Vermont and at Peters Valley Craft Center in Layton, NJ.

Burton is the department leader for the Technology Education program at Boyertown Area Senior High School. This is his fourth book for Popular Woodworking.

ACKNOWLEDGEMENTS

Many people are involved in bringing a book to life, and this one is no exception. As with the other projects I've been involved with, my family — wife Susan and daughters Sarah and Emma — endured a lot of long evenings and weekends with me routing away in the shop, and pecking away at the keyboard.

Jeff Day pitched in, sanding everything in sight and fitting drawers as deadlines loomed large. Donna Chiarelli lent her skills as a photographer to give the project shots at the beginning of each chapter a special touch. And the team at F & W publications—Jim Stack, David Thiel, and Brain Roeth—pitched in to pull the whole mess together and make it look as good as it does. Thanks fellas.

Missing from the photos is Jared Haas, who was Mr. Hands for my first two books. He made up for this by being the guy behind the camera and guiding force in getting the DVD put together.

On the commercial side, my hat is off to J. R. Weber at Eagle America, Jason Feldner, at Bosch Power Tools, and Dan Sherman at JessEm Tool Company for providing many of the tools and tooling that I used as I was building the projects herein. You guys are the best!

contents

introduction

I still have vivid memories of the first time I used a router. I had pooled my money with my father and we had brought home one of Sears Best (in those days, perennially on sale for $1/2$ price) along with a starter kit of steel bits. I chucked up a $3/8$-inch straight bit and went to town on a scrap of red oak. When the smoke and dust cleared, and my ears quit ringing (who knew the thing would be quite that loud?). I stood back to admire the jagged cut I had created across the face of the board. Not very impressive.

In talking with people at the various workshops I've taught, that kind of router experience is not uncommon. In fact, it is the kind of thing that makes many people put their router on a shelf and leave it there to gather dust (instead of making it!). Fortunately, I wasn't quite that discouraged. Plus, I was lucky enough to have friends and teachers, along with a pile of good books and magazines, who were willing to show me how to use a router to good advantage. In the years since, I've come to rely on routers for almost everything I build. In fact, I am convinced that you can build almost anything out of wood if you have access to a router and a table saw. (Not that I'm quite willing to give up the rest of my machinery.)

The Secrets to Good Routing

So what are the secrets to routing success? They are actually very simple. The first is to know when to use a handheld router versus when to use a table-mounted one. The key here is to think about the piece you are trying to cut. If it is easier to move the workpiece (which it often is with smaller pieces), you should probably think table-mounted router. If it is easier to move the router (larger workpieces) then go with the handheld tool. You could get two routers to give yourself this flexibility, although you can simply attach your handheld router to the underside of your router table when you need a table-mounted router. I worked this way for years. However, what I recommend is that you purchase one of the router kits that come with two bases – a fixed base which you can mount to your router table, and a plunge base that you can use for handheld applications. Being able to swap the motor back and forth saves considerable amounts of time.

The second secret is to provide some means of guiding the router. This can be as simple as a straight piece of wood that you guide the router along, or as elaborate a jig as you care to make. I've included plans for a number of jigs that I use all the time and have tried to show how each is used. Some of these are fairly universal (like the mortising jig), and can be used again and again, while others are made specifically for a certain project (although the concepts involved are adaptable to other situations).

The third secret is to consider the rotation of the bit as you make your cuts. On a router

table, this usually means cutting from right to left. This way, the rotation of the bit pushes the work against the fence. With a handheld router, you will usually cut from left to right if the router is between you and the work and from right to left if the work is between you and the router.

The final secret is to take small bites. Routers are wonderful tools and can be made to do almost anything, but they don't do well if you try to remove too much material at once. So the key here is either to cut away most of the excess with some other tool first, or to make the cut in several shallow passes. The only times I've ever had real difficulties with a router have been when I didn't follow this last guideline.

Buying a Router

If you're only going to buy a single router, get one with a 1.5 to 2 horsepower motor and a plunge base. This size router is powerful enough for most work yet not so heavy as to be difficult to maneuver. The plunge base

is particularly handy for cutting mortises. As I mentioned above, what are nice are the kits that come with two bases — fixed and plunge — so you can attach one of the bases under a router table and swap the motor in between. I used Bosch routers to build all the pieces in this book and have been really impressed with them. I have also had good luck with my Elu (now Dewalt) and Hitachi (the replacement for my original "Sears Best") plunge routers.

Router Bits

You won't have to do many projects before you'll have invested more in your bit collection than you have in your router. I do recommend you invest in carbide-tipped bits. Steel bits, while considerably less expensive, just don't stay sharp long enough to be serviceable; and dull bits will quickly scorch your work. There are a number of companies that sell router bits. One I deal with frequently is Eagle America. They have a great selection and are nice

folks to deal with. I've listed their catalog numbers for the bits I used for each project to make it easier for you to obtain the necessary tooling. However, don't be afraid to use the bits you already have — a $3/8$-inch straight bit is a $3/8$-inch straight bit no matter what the source. Also, you may be able to substitute one bit for another. I often use a 1" straight bit for trim cuts while a $7/8$" or even a $3/4$" bit would work just as well.

Router Tables

Until this past year, I worked exclusively with router tables I had made. My first was a piece of $3/4$" plywood I simply screwed the router to. I placed this over a trash can (dust collection at its best!) and routed away. I have built several tables since then. I was looking to upgrade my latest shop-made creation with a lift (a router holding mechanism that allows you to adjust the bit height from the top of the table) when I was offered a commercial router table (with a lift) from the JessEm

Tool Company. I decided to give it a try and have been favorably impressed. The lift works quite well and makes precision adjustments a breeze, and the fence is a joy to use. If you have the funds, purchasing such a table is a good alternative to building one of your own.

About the Projects

I hope you have fun building the projects in this book and come away knowing a little more about using the router. I designed each piece with certain techniques in mind, and tried to include many of the jigs I find most useful in day-to-day woodworking. In taking the photographs, I tried to include as much detail as I could without getting bogged down in showing processes common to every project (cutting stock to size, etc). Please don't hesitate to contact me if you run into problems, or have suggestions for improvement.

routed boxes

ROUTED BOXES are a lot of fun to make, they go together quickly, so you can make them up in batches without investing tons of time. They don't require a lot of materials. And they offer some unique design opportunities in terms of shapes and profiles that are possible.

Unlike traditional boxes, where you cut joints to fasten separate pieces of wood together, both of these routed boxes were fashioned by routing out the interior of a solid chunk of wood.

The body of the cherry and walnut box was cut from a relatively long length of cherry that had been routed with a tray bit. Thus, you can make this style of box as short or as long as you want it.

The other box was made with the help of templates. Once you get the hang of making the templates, you'll be able to make any number of different boxes using the same basic processes. Then you can branch out into other decorative techniques, such as inlay.

WENGE AND MAPLE BOX

inches (millimeters)

REFERENCE	QUANTITY	PART	STOCK	THICKNESS	(mm)	WIDTH	(mm)	LENGTH	(mm)
A	1	body	hardwood	1	(25)	3	(76)	5 1/2	(140)
B	1	lid	hardwood	7/16	(11)	2 1/4	(57)	4 3/4	(121)
C	2	feet	hardwood	1/8	(3)	5/16	(8)	2 5/8	(67)
D	1	stringing	hardwood	1/16	(2)	1/16	(2)	9	(229)
E	1	plug 1	hardwood			5/8 D	(16)	1/4	(6)
F	1	plug 2	hardwood			3/8 D	(10)	1/4	(6)

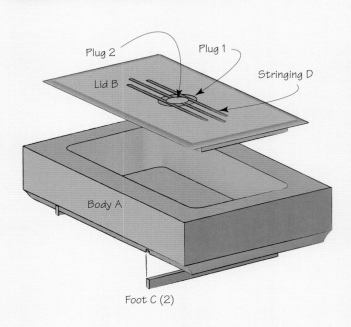

Plug 2
Plug 1
Lid B
Stringing D
Body A
Foot C (2)

BIT BOX

EAGLE AMERICA CATALOG NO.

1/2" straight, 1/2" shank, No. 102-0885

1/8" straight, 1/4" shank, No. 102-0202

3/8" roundover, 1/2" shank, No. 156-0605

5/8" cove, 1/2" shank, No. 154-1005

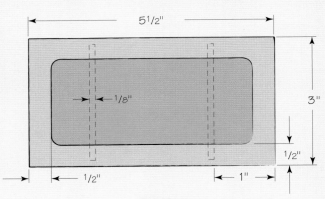

5 1/2"

1/8"

3"

1/2"

1/2"

1"

Top view

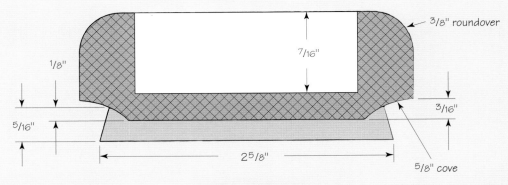

3/8" roundover

7/16"

1/8"

3/16"

5/16"

2 5/8"

5/8" cove

Side Cross Section

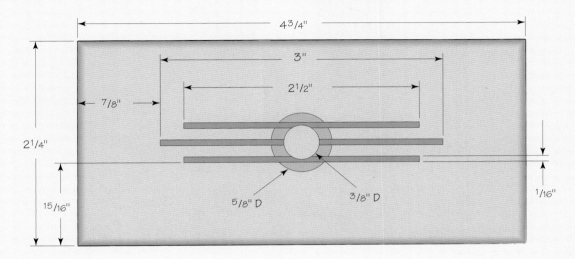

43/4"

3"

21/2"

7/8"

21/4"

15/16"

5/8" D

3/8" D

1/16"

Top Detail

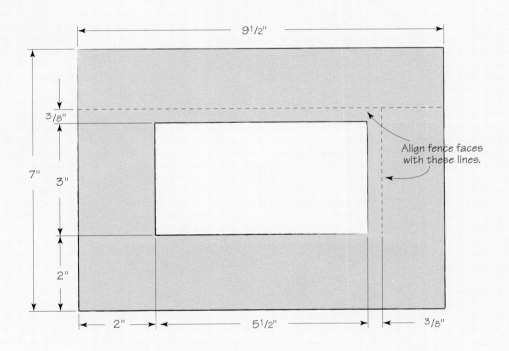

91/2"

3/8"

7"

3"

2"

2"

51/2"

3/8"

Align fence faces
with these lines.

Template Detail

ROUTED BOXES

STEP 1 Cut the pieces for the box body, top, and template to size. Lay out the outline of the body on the template — the lines should be 2" in from the edges as shown in the Template Detail. Then, lay out the cut lines on the template. These lines should be 3/8" inside the first lines.

STEP 2 Locate the fence on your table saw 2³/8" from the blade. Lower the blade beneath the table. Place the template over the blade opening with one of the short sides against the fence and hold it securely. (Note: Keep your fingers away from the layout lines — this is where the blade will appear.) Turn on the saw and carefully raise the blade until it cuts through the template. Keep raising the blade until the cut extends from one cut line to the other. Lower the blade.

STEP 3 Reverse the piece to cut the second short side. Then cut the first long side. When you cut the long sides, you may need to push the template along the fence a little bit to complete the cuts. Before you cut the second long side, screw a scrap to the template and the cutout part in the center to prevent the cutout from kicking back when it is cut free. (Note: Don't worry about overcutting the corners, it won't affect the way the template functions.)

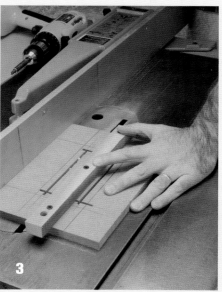

STEP 4 Cut a length of scrap about 1" × 2" × 12" to serve as a fence. Cut about 2" off the end of the scrap and screw this short piece to the face of the longer one. Fasten the fence to the underside of the template with double-sided tape, aligning it with the outer layout lines you drew earlier. Screw the fence in place from the opposite side of the template.

STEP 5 Load the box body onto the template, then grip the entire assembly in a vise. As you tighten the vise, make sure the template is seated firmly down on top of the box.

STEP 6 Install a 3/4" outside diameter template guide on your plunge router along with a 1/2" spiral upcut or straight bit. Set the stop to limit the depth of cut to 3/4". Rout out the interior of the box in several passes. You may find it helpful to vacuum out the chips periodically as you go.

STEP 7 Chuck a 1/8" straight bit in your table-mounted router and set its height to make a 1/8" deep cut. Use the fence to locate the dadoes 1" in from the ends as shown in the Top View. Cut the dadoes across the bottom of the box for the feet. With relatively narrow pieces such as this, it helps to guide them along the fence with the aid of a push block. A push block helps keep the piece square to the fence, and it helps prevent tear-out when cutting across the grain as it supports the wood fibers where the bit exits.

Precise Depth Settings

If you need to set your router to cut to a specific depth, start by lowering the bit until it touches the surface into which you'll be routing. This establishes a zero point. Then, use a drill bit of the appropriate diameter to set the depth stop. You'll get amazing accuracy with a minimum of fuss.

STEP 8 To cut the profiles on the box, you'll need to position the fence so the bits are partially behind the working surface. Many commercial fences slide open to allow this configuration. (You can achieve the same thing in a solid wood fence simply by cutting a notch for the bit.) Use a straightedge to position the fence tangent to the bit's guide bearing.

STEP 9 Rout a $^3/_8$"-radius roundover around the top edges of the box (photo 9A) and a $^5/_8$"-diameter cove around the bottom (photo 9B) as shown in the Side Cross Section. For both of these profiles, cut across the ends of the box first with the aid of a push block. Then rout the long sides. Routing across the grain first allows any tearout to be cut away when you make the second set of cuts.

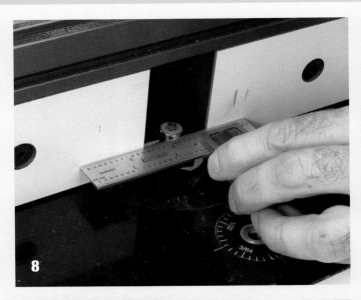

Push Blocks

I don't invest a lot of time or effort making push blocks. Usually I'll just grab a scrap of MDF or plywood and use it as is (as long as the corners are square). If you start with a fresh block, you'll have eight corners you can rout before you either discard the push block, or cut it down to expose fresh corners.

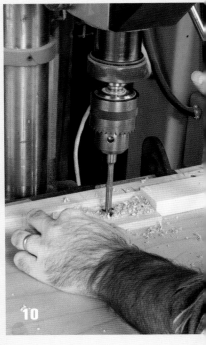

STEP 10 Cut the box top to size and draw diagonals across it to locate the center. Before drilling the lid, use a $^5/_8$"-plug cutter to cut a plug from a piece of contrasting wood. Then set up fences and drill a $^5/_8$" hole, $^1/_4$" deep at the lid's center point. Leave the positioning fences in place — you'll need them again when you drill a hole for the second plug. Glue the $^5/_8$" plug in the hole and sand it flush.

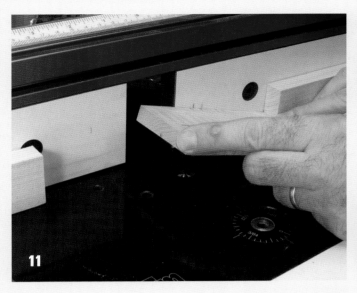

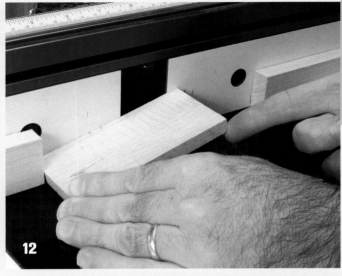

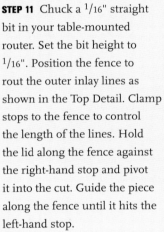

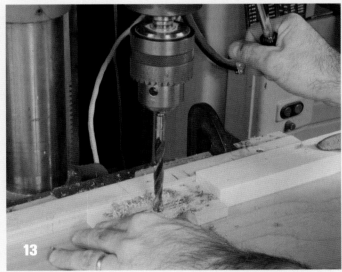

STEP 11 Chuck a $1/16$" straight bit in your table-mounted router. Set the bit height to $1/16$". Position the fence to rout the outer inlay lines as shown in the Top Detail. Clamp stops to the fence to control the length of the lines. Hold the lid along the fence against the right-hand stop and pivot it into the cut. Guide the piece along the fence until it hits the left-hand stop.

STEP 12 When the lid touches the left-hand stop, pivot it up away from the bit. Turn the lid around and rout the second outside line. Then reposition the fence and the stops and cut the center line. (Note: Getting the center line truly centered takes some fussing. I usually try to have some scraps on hand that are the same dimensions as my good material so I can make some test cuts.)

STEP 13 Square the ends of the routed lines with a chisel. (I ground a spare $1/8$" chisel down especially for this purpose.) Cut lengths of black stringing to fit in the lines. Glue them in place and sand everything flush. Go back to the drill press and drill a $3/8$" hole in the center of the lid, using the same fences as you did to drill the original hole. Cut a $3/8$" plug from a scrap of the lid material and glue it in the hole.

STEP 14 Round over the top edges of the lid with a $5/16$" round over bit. As always, cut across the ends of the lid first, then do the sides to clean up any tear-out.

STEP 15 Set up a large ($1/2$" to 1") diameter straight bit in your table-mounted router. Set the depth of cut to about $1/8$". Position the fence to expose slightly less than $1/8$" of the bit. Cut a rabbet around all four edges on the underside of the lid. Test the fit of the lid in the box. (Note: It won't go in perfectly until you round the corners — you just want to make sure the fit is good from end to end and side to side.) If necessary, bump the fence over to expose a little more of the bit to make the rabbet a little wider. You want a little bit less than $1/16$" of clearance in both directions.

STEP 16 Once you have the rabbets cut to the right width, cut the corners round with a sharp chisel. Trace around a circle template to give yourself guidelines for the cuts.

STEP 17 Cut the feet to size and cut their ends at an angle as shown in the Side Cross Section. Glue the feet into the dadoes you routed earlier.

STEP 18 Sand everything, then finish the box with your favorite finish. To finish the inside, consider using flocking. Flocking is a little like powdered fabric — paint the surfaces you want to coat, then sprinkle the flocking over the wet paint. Once all the wet paint is covered with the flocking, you can dump out the excess. They sell special flocking guns, but I've always had good luck simply pouring the material right from the bag. If I'm making multiple pieces, I'll simply pour the excess from one right into the next.

WALNUT AND CHERRY BOX

inches (millimeters)

REFERENCE	QUANTITY	PART	STOCK	THICKNESS	(mm)	WIDTH	(mm)	LENGTH	(mm)	COMMENTS
A	1	body	hardwood	1	(25)	$2^1/2$	(64)	13	(330)	length is for 3 boxes
B	1	lid	hardwood	$^1/2$	(13)	$2^1/2$	(64)	17	(432)	length is for 3 boxes
C	2	ends	hardwood	$^1/4$	(6)	$1^9/16$	(40)	17	(432)	length is for 3 boxes
D	2	pivot pins	hardwood			$^1/8$D	(3)	1	(25)	

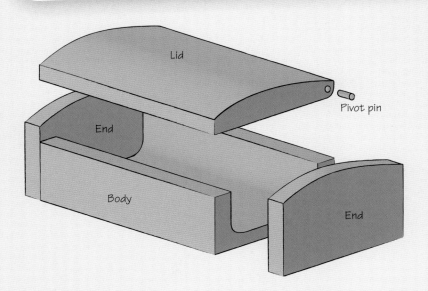

BIT BOX

EAGLE AMERICA CATALOG NO.
tray/bowl, $^1/2$" shank, No.144-1205
furniture maker, $^1/2$" shank, No.162-2015
$^3/16$" roundover, $^1/2$" shank, No.156-0305

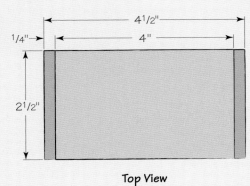

Top View

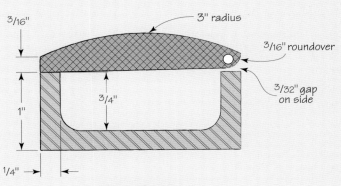

Cross Section

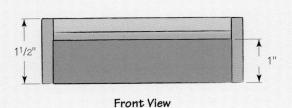

Front View

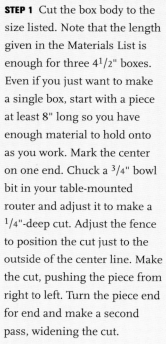

STEP 1 Cut the box body to the size listed. Note that the length given in the Materials List is enough for three $4^1/2$" boxes. Even if you just want to make a single box, start with a piece at least 8" long so you have enough material to hold onto as you work. Mark the center on one end. Chuck a $3/4$" bowl bit in your table-mounted router and adjust it to make a $1/4$"-deep cut. Adjust the fence to position the cut just to the outside of the center line. Make the cut, pushing the piece from right to left. Turn the piece end for end and make a second pass, widening the cut.

STEP 2 Raise the bit $1/4$" to make the cut deeper. Again make two passes. Raise the bit another $1/4$" to finish the cut. (Note: when you make the second pass at each depth, only half of the bit is actually in contact with the wood.) In this situation, if the material being cut is between the fence and the bit, the bit's rotation will tend to pull the piece out of your hands if you feed it from right to left. However, if you feed it in the opposite direction, left to right, the bit will tend to push the piece away from the fence. This is why it is important to make the set up with the bit to the side of the center line that is away from the fence. In this configuration, you can make the cut from right to left without either of the problems I just mentioned.

STEP 3 Once the cut is at full depth, move the fence about $1/8$" away from the bit. Make two passes to widen the cut on both sides. Repeat as needed until the walls are $1/4$"-thick. Depending on your initial set up, you may have a small lump in the center of the cut. If this is the case, reposition the fence to cut it away. As long as you don't change the bit height, this should smooth everything out.

STEP 4 Cut the material for the lid to the size specified. (Note: It is several inches longer than the piece for the box body as you'll need a little extra length for the top profile cuts.) Attach a length of scrap to the backside of the piece to serve as a handle. I stuck my handle on with double-faced tape.(You'll only need about 2" of tape at either end. I find that if I squeeze the taped connection with a clamp, it is more than secure enough. If you don't have any tape, or don't like the idea, you can glue the scrap in place. Again, you'll only need to glue about 2" at either end.

STEP 5 Chuck a furniture maker's bit in your table-mounted router and adjust its height so the bearing is just above the center of the lid. Adjust the fence so it is tangent to the guide bearing.

STEP 6 Draw lines on the edges of the top about 2" in from either end. Start the cut by pivoting the piece against the fence, so the line on the leading end aligns with the opening in the fence to the left of the bit. Once the piece is in contact with the fence, push it from right to left.

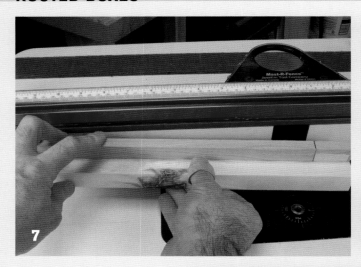

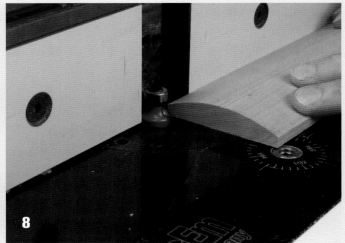

STEP 7 Stop cutting when the line near the trailing end reaches the opening to the right of the bit. Pivot the piece away from the fence. Turn the piece over and repeat the process to cut the second part of the profile. Leaving a little uncut material at either end gives the piece plenty of support against the fence.

STEP 8 Chuck a 3/16" roundover bit in your table-mounted router and round over one of the **bott**om edges of the lid. This will provide clearance so the lid can open.

STEP 9 Sand and finish the inside of the body piece. It is much easier to do it when the piece is still long. Cut both the box body and lid to length on the table saw. Guide the pieces past the blade with the miter gauge. Position a stop to control the length of the pieces. Cut all the pieces with the same setup so they all end up the same length.

STEP 10 Cut a piece for the sides to the size given in the Materials List. Then crosscut the individual side pieces to length, leaving them about 1/16" longer than the width of the box body. Carefully sand the inside face of each side piece. Try not to round over the edges at all. Glue the ends to the body so their bottom edges are flush with the bottom of the body. The extra length gives you a little margin for error from front to back.

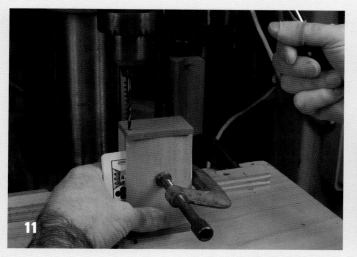

STEP 11 When the glue dries, slide the top into place. You may need to sand its ends a little to get it to fit. Sandwich three or four playing cards in between the pieces before you clamp them together. (Make sure the back edge of the top is flush with the back of the body — you can trim any overlap in front later.) Having the cards in place when you drill for the hinge pins provides the necessary clearance for the lid to open without binding. Lay out the hole locations as shown in the Side View. Double-check to make sure the holes will end up in the right place on the lid as shown in the Cross Section (page 17).

STEP 12 Push the pivot pins into their holes to locate the lid. Trace the curve of the lid onto the sides. Cut down close to the lines with a sharp chisel. Reassemble the box and sand the lid and sides to make them flush.

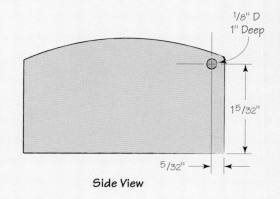

STEP 13 Start the pivot pins into their holes. When about $1/4$" remains exposed, wipe a little glue on and drive it home. Sand away any excess dowel and glue. Also, go over the whole piece with fine sandpaper. Finish the box as you see fit. The box in the photo has the gentle luster of a hand-rubbed, oil finish.

$1/8$" D
1" Deep

$1^5/32$"

$5/32$"

Side View

Fitting Dowels as Pivot Pins

Fitting a length of $1/8$" dowel into a $1/8$" hole can be tricky, especially if the dowel is slightly oversize. I found an easy way to reduce a dowel's diameter is to chuck it in an electric drill and sand it as the drill is spinning. When I made the pins for the box, I actually made them taper a little with this method. I wanted the part of the dowel that went into the lid to be slightly undersize so the lid could pivot easily. And, I wanted the part that fit into the sides to be a snug fit so I could glue it in place.

clock

I HAVE ALWAYS ENJOYED designing clocks because their faces' provide a great opportunity to play around with inlays and other graphic elements. This clock is no exception. Its face features a bookmatched sycamore veneer surface inlaid with a ring of ebony stringing and a purpleheart dot. Its asymmetrical form contrasts nicely with the geometric precision of the ellipses that make up the base.

Speaking of the ellipses, they were made with assistance from a set of commercial ellipse templates. While you can make up your own templates, buying a set takes a lot of the hassle out of creating these elegant shapes. Once you make the various ellipse-shaped pieces for the clock base, you can cut the decorative profiles around their edges with a selection of edge-forming bits. The profiles on the base and plinth are "stock" — that is they are created by using a specific bit. The third (around the collar) is more unique. It is created with a small chamfer bit used in a somewhat unconventional manner. The column itself also has an elliptical profile, although this is created with a router bit (the same one used on the base) rather than a template.

Along with all the decorative router cuts is a little joinery. The pieces are all mortised and are joined with loose tenons. The mortises are all cut with the router, as are the roundovers on the tenons' edges.

In all, this was a fun piece to make, and building it may give you a chance to expand your woodworking horizons.

CLOCK
inches (millimeters)

REFERENCE	QUANTITY	PART	STOCK	THICKNESS	(mm)	WIDTH	(mm)	LENGTH	(mm)
A	1	head substrate	hardwood	7/8	(22)	9 5/8	(244)	7 1/2	(191)
B	4	veneers	hardwood	3/32	(2.5)	5	(127)	8	(203)
C	1	collar	hardwood	1/2	(13)	3 7/16	(87)	4 7/8	(124)
D	1	plinth	hardwood	5/8	(16)	2 9/16	(65)	4	(102)
E	1	base	hardwood	7/8	(22)	5 7/8	(149)	7 7/8	(200)
F	1	column	hardwood	1 1/8	(29)	2 3/8	(60)	7	(178)
G	2	tenons	hardwood	3/8	(10)	1 1/4	(32)	2 1/8	(54)
H	1	stringing	hardwood	1/16	(2)	1/16	(2)	15	(381)
J	1	plug	hardwood			5/8 D	(16)	1/4	(6)
K	1	small template	MDF	1/2	(12)	4	(102)	5	(127)
L	1	template	MDF	1/2	(12)	9	(229)	11	(279)
M	1	template	MDF	1/2	(12)	10	(254)	10	(254)
N	1	clock movement							

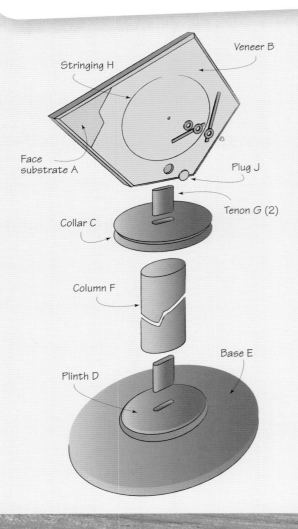

Stringing H
Veneer B
Face substrate A
Plug J
Collar C
Tenon G (2)
Column F
Plinth D
Base E

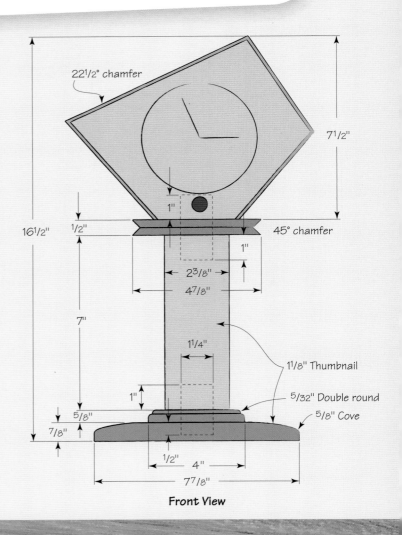

22 1/2° chamfer
7 1/2"
1"
16 1/2"
1/2"
45° chamfer
2 3/8"
4 7/8"
1"
7"
1 1/4"
1 1/8" Thumbnail
5/32" Double round
5/8" Cove
1"
5/8"
7/8"
1/2"
4"
7 7/8"

Front View

BIT BOX

EAGLE AMERICA CATALOG NO.

flush trim, 1/2" shank,
No. 117-0825

3/8" straight, 1/2" shank,
No. 102-0645

5/32" double round, 1/2" shank,
No. 169-2705

45° chamfer, 1/2" shank,
No. 152-0625

thumbnail, 1/2" shank,
No. 174-4005

5/8" cove, 1/2" shank,
No. 154-1005

1/2" straight, 1/2" shank,
No. 102-0845

1/16" straight, 1/4" shank,
No. 102-0102

22.5° chamfer, 1/2" shank,
No. 152-0305

3/16" roundover, 1/2" shank,
No. 156-0305

5/8" template guide

5/8" Forstner bit

5/8" plug cutter

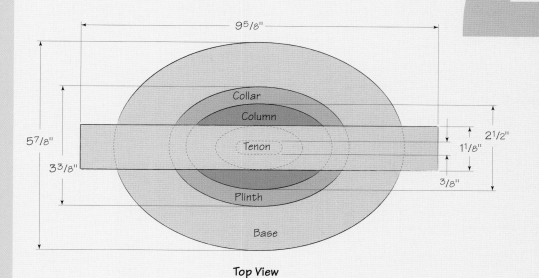

Top View

1

STEP 1 I resawed a piece of quartersawn sycamore to create the veneers for the clock's face, but you can also purchase veneers that are ready to apply. Regardless of which way you go, you'll need to match the veneers along one edge or the other to create the bookmatched appearance shown. When bookmatching veneers, you simply hold consecutive pieces together and open them like a book. With the sycamore I was using, I could either have matched the veneers along their dark edges, or along their lighter edge. I chose to put the lighter match in the center. (Note, as you're selecting your veneers, be sure to cut them slightly longer and wider than the substrate you'll be gluing them to.)

STEP 2 Once you've decided on your match, you'll need to make the adjoining edges nice and straight so they'll go together flawlessly. To accomplish this, you'll need to make a simple veneer clamping/jointing jig. This is essentially two straight pieces of MDF or plywood that can be bolted together with the veneers in between. My version is shown in photos 2 and 3. To use the jig, align the veneers on the bottom board with their adjoining edges projecting about 1/16" past the edge. Set the top board in place and tighten the knobs.

STEP 3 Trim the edges of the veneer straight and true with a flush-trim bit in your table-mounted router.

STEP 4 Before gluing the veneers to their substrate, tape them together along the edges you just routed. (While you can get a special paper veneer tape, ordinary masking tape works almost as well and is a lot more readily available.) Fasten the tape to one veneer and stretch it across the joint to fasten it to the other. Masking tape is surprisingly elastic and stretches well. By stretching the tape, you'll add a little pressure across the joint that will help keep the veneers together.

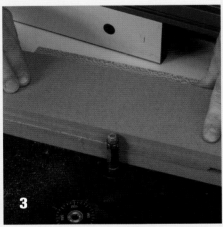

Veneer Clamping/Jointing Jig

Getting straight edges on two or more pieces of veneer can be tricky. What you need is a device that can serve both as a guide for your router as well as a clamp for the veneer. This simple jig serves both purposes. The two outer boards are fastened together with studded knobs and T-nuts. There are two sets of homes so you can use the jig with different lengths of material.

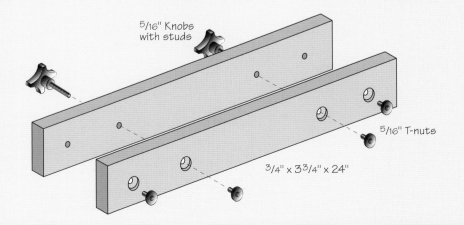

5/16" Knobs with studs

5/16" T-nuts

3/4" x 3³/4" x 24"

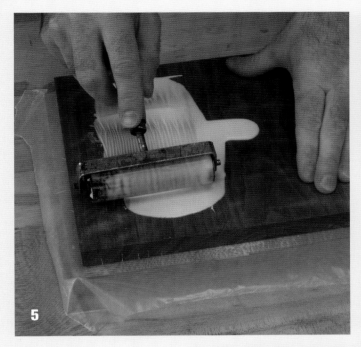

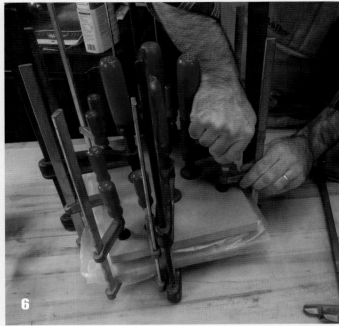

STEP 5 Cut the head substrate about 3/8" larger than you need in both directions. Also cut two pieces of MDF or other flat sheet stock to serve as cauls. Place one of these cauls on your bench and cover it with waxed paper. Place one of the veneer panels on the waxed paper, tape-side down. Apply glue to the substrate and place the substrate on the veneer. Apply glue to second side of the substrate, then add the second veneer panel, more waxed paper and the second caul. (Note: The best tool I've found for spreading glue in this situation is a small printers brayer, basically a hard rubber roller.)

STEP 6 Clamp the whole sandwich together and set it aside to dry.

STEP 7 Cut the pieces for the collar, plinth and base to size. Carefully lay out center lines across all three pieces. These will help you align the ellipse templates on the pieces, as well as help you cut the mortises in the right places.

Gluing Veneer

When gluing up veneered panels, only apply glue to the substrate. If you apply the glue to the veneer it will curl up from the added moisture. Once this happens, it's almost impossible to get it to lie flat enough to clamp up.

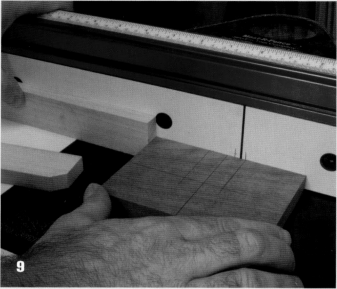

STEP 8 Chuck a $3/8$" spiral upcut (or straight) bit in your table-mounted router to cut the mortises. Adjust the fence so the bit will cut right in the center of the collar. Hold the collar against the fence and butt it up against the bit. Make two marks on the fence to indicate the bit's location as shown.

STEP 9 Draw two lines on the collar $5/8$" on either side of the center line to indicate the length of the mortise. Lower the bit beneath the surface of the table. Hold the collar against the fence and align the mortise end lines with the marks on the fence. Clamp stops to the fence to control the length of the mortise. (Note: Cut a small bevel on the ends of the stops. This provides room for chips to build up where they won't interfere with the motion of the workpiece.)

STEP 10 Raise the bit so it makes a cut about $5/16$" deep. Hold the collar at an angle against the fence and against the right-hand stop. Start the router and pivot the collar down along the fence until it is flat on the table. Feed the collar along the fence until it touches the left-hand stop.

STEP 11 When the collar touches the left-hand stop, pivot it up along the fence and off of the bit. Turn the piece over and repeat the process with the same edge against the fence. The photos show making the second cut. If necessary, raise the bit and repeat the process until the mortise is cut all the way through the collar. Reset the fence and cut a mortise through the plinth in the same manner. Also mortise the base, but only from the top side. Make the mortise 1/2" deep.

STEP 12 Once the mortises are cut in the base, collar and plinth, you can cut the three pieces to shape. Trace the ellipses on them and cut them roughly to size on the band saw, staying about 1/16" from the line. Fasten the templates to the blanks with double-faced tape. Rout the pieces to their final shape with a flush trim bit.

The white piece to the right of the bit is called a starting pin. It is handy for starting a cut when you cannot use the fence. Hold the workpiece against the starting pin, then slowly pivot it into the cut. Once the piece is against the bit's guide bearing you don't have to keep it against the starting pin. In the photo, I'm actually cutting on the side opposite the starting pin as the chips tended to go toward the dust pick up. (Note: While the collar can be routed using a

standard template, the plinth and the base require templates that are slightly smaller than the ones that come with the kit.) These can be easily made as shown in Making Your Own Ellipse Sizes.

STEP 13 Rout the double roundover profile around the top edge of the plinth. Rather than using the starting pin, I've positioned the fence close enough to the bit that I can pivot off the fence's corner to get things started. Having the fence this close to the bit lets me use the fence's built-in dust collection port. (Note: The piece to the right is just there to show what the profile looks like. It should NOT be there when you are actually cutting.)

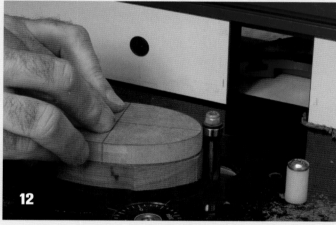

Making Your Own Ellipse Sizes

While I really like the commercial ellipse template set, I don't want to be trapped into only making the size ellipses that came with it. Fortunately, it is fairly simple to make your own custom templates using the kit as a starting point.

One way to make intermediate size ellipses is to set up a router with a straight bit and a guide bushing. Depending on the combination of bit and bushing you choose, you can increase or decrease the size of the ellipse accordingly. (Note: the templates are stuck down to a piece of MDF which is being routed to make an intermediate size of ellipse.) The smaller template is just there to help balance the router.

When great precision isn't an issue, you can quickly trace one of the templates, then cut out the resulting ellipse on the band saw and sand it smooth. Various sizes of washers will give you a good range of options to choose from.

STEP 14 Swap the double roundover bit for a small chamfer bit. Raise the bit until the outer tip is at the midpoint of the collar. Make the first cut with the bearing on the bit riding against the ellipse template. Fasten the template to the other side of the collar and repeat the procedure. (The photo shows starting this second cut, the piece to the right is there to show what the profile is supposed to look like.)

STEP 15 Cut a $5/8"$ cove around the bottom edge of the base.

STEP 16 Round over the top edge of the base with a thumbnail bit. This is a large diameter bit and should be run at a slower speed (12,000 RPM$^+$/-). Make the cut in several passes, raising the bit a little each time.

STEP 17 While you have the thumbnail bit in the router, use it to cut the column to its elliptical profile. Start by cutting the column to the listed thickness and width, but leave the piece 5" too long for now. If you have to glue pieces together to achieve the proper thickness, consider adding a thin piece of contrasting wood in the middle as I did. Draw lines around the blank, 1" in from the ends. Set up the fence so its faces are tangent to the bit's bearing. Start the cut by pivoting the piece into the fence so the line on the leading end touches the fence at the end of the gap to the left of the bit. Feed the piece along the fence and pivot away from the bit when the line at the trailing end reaches the gap to the right of the bit.

STEP 18 Cut the column to length. The piece is wide enough that there should be a small flat on both the front and back faces. Clamp the column to the mortising jig (For plans, see Mortising Jig on page 36). Using the same bit you used to mortise the base, plinth and collar, cut a 1 1/4"-long mortise in both ends of the column. The mortise should be centered from side to side and front to back.

17A

17B

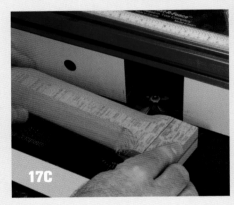

17C

STEP 19 Unclamp the head and trim it to final size. Be sure to cut a little off each side to trim away any glue squeeze out. Lay out the angled cuts as shown in the Head Detail. Also lay out the location of the hole at the center of the clock face.

18

19

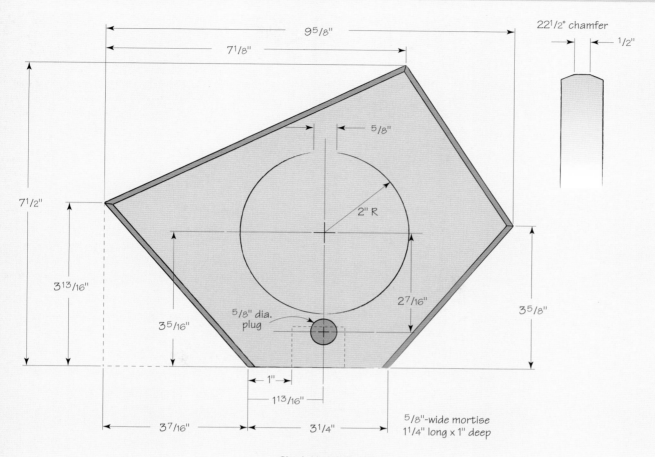

22¹/₂° chamfer

1/2"

9⁵/₈"

7¹/₈"

5/8"

2" R

7¹/₂"

3¹³/₁₆"

3⁵/₁₆"

2⁷/₁₆"

3⁵/₈"

5/8" dia. plug

1"

1¹³/₁₆"

3⁷/₁₆"

3¹/₄"

5/8"-wide mortise
1¹/₄" long x 1" deep

Clock Head Detail

20A

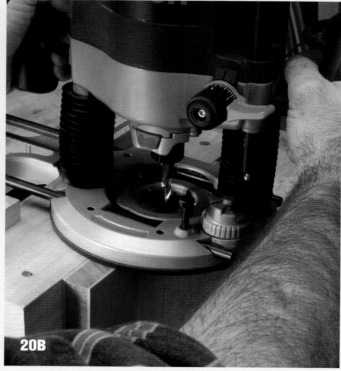

20B

STEP 20 Clamp the head to the front of the mortising jig with its bottom edge flush with the top of the jig. You won't be able to use the jig's fences, so you'll have to rely on regular clamps. If this proves troublesome, you can always drive screws through the waste areas of the head into the face of the jig. Mortise the head with the same bit you used to cut the other mortises. Center the mortise from front to back. Locate it from side to side as shown in the Clock Head Detail.

STEP 21 Drill a $5/16$" hole through the head at the center of the clock face. Insert the movement's shaft through the hole from the back. Square the movement to the head and trace around it to mark the location of the mortise.

STEP 22 Make up a template with a cut out big enough for the movement plus the appropriate offset for your combination of bit and template guide. I used a $1/2$" bit and a $5/8$" template guide. You can make the cutout on the table saw. There are photos detailing this on page 12. Rout the mortise for the clock. Leave the clock face about $3/16$" thick. Make the cut in several passes, pausing to vacuum out the chips occasionally.

STEP 23 Chuck a $1/16$" straight bit in a plunge router with an attached trammel. (See A Small Router Trammel on page 67.) Set the radius to $2^1/8$" and set the depth of cut to slightly less than $1/16$". Mark the start and stop points on the clock face as shown in the Head Detail. Place the trammel's pivot in the hole at the center of the clock face. Cut the circular groove for the inlay, being careful to start and stop the cut precisely at your marks.

21

22

23

Template Tip

When you make up a template for a cut you might make again — such as the mortise for a clock movement — write the key information right on the template. This might include what bit and template guide combination to use, what size mortise the template makes, etc.

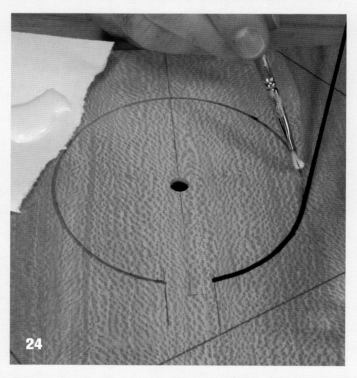

24

STEP 24 Trim the ends of the circular groove square. I ground down a spare chisel to deal with such small tasks. Apply glue to the first few inches of the groove and press the stringing into place. The round bulb on the end of a screw driver handle makes a good tool for seating the inlay. I was a little worried about breaking the piece as I forced it around the tight radius. However, I was pleasantly surprised to find that by seating the stringing as I went, even a brittle wood such as ebony could be forced to cooperate. Work your way around the circle, and trim the end of the stringing to fit.

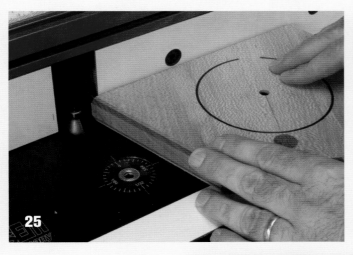

25

26

STEP 25 Cut the head to shape on the band saw and sand the sawn edges straight. Chuck a 22.5° chamfer bit in your table-mounted router and cut chamfers around all but the bottom edge. Adjust the height of the bit to leave about a $1/2$" flat on the edge between the chamfers.

27

STEP 26 I find a sanding mop makes short work of sanding the profiles on small pieces such as these clock parts. The feathery strips of abrasive smooth the imperfections away without drastically altering the profile.

STEP 27 Cut a length of tenon stock to the proper width and thickness. Round over the corners with a $3/16$" roundover bit. Cut the two tenons to length to join the base and plinth to the column, and the column to the collar and head.

STEP 28 Finish the pieces separately, then get ready to glue them together. Cut an angled clamping block to fit over the top of the head. Swab glue in the mortises and on the tenons. Assemble all the pieces and clamp the whole thing together.

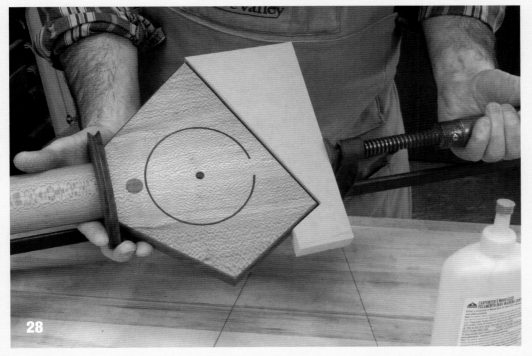

28

A Mortising Jig and Edge Guide

Of all the router jigs I've made, the one that I use the most is my mortising jig. I made the original version of this jig about 19 years ago and have been revising it ever since. In fact, as I was putting this book together, I made a couple of improvements to it, so you may notice some differences in the photos from one project to the next.

The jig is essentially a means of holding on to a workpiece so you can rout it. To this end, there are two fences that bolt to the front of the jig. One is a horizontal fence for holding pieces so you can mortise their edges, the other is a vertical fence so you can cut mortises in the pieces' ends.

The jig also incorporates adjustable stops to make cutting the mortise to the right size easy, and they help insure repeatability if you are making multiple pieces with the same joinery.

The jig is designed to work with a plunge router equipped with an edge guide. While you can purchase an edge guide, I have included plans for one you can make. This is worth considering because one of the improvements I've made to the jig is a fence extension that interlocks with the fence on the shop-made edge guide and helps prevent the router from tipping as you work.

Most of the jig is made from 8/4 hardwood. I used ash for

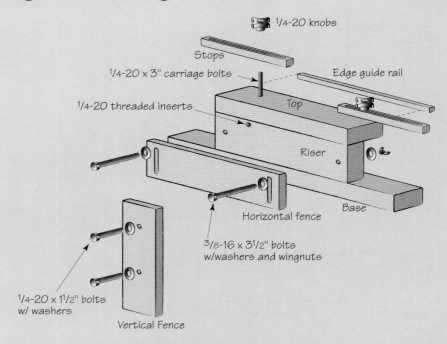

¹/4-20 knobs

Stops

¹/4-20 x 3" carriage bolts

¹/4-20 threaded inserts

Edge guide rail

Top

Riser

Base

Horizontal fence

³/8-16 x 3¹/2" bolts
w/washers and wingnuts

¹/4-20 x 1¹/2" bolts
w/ washers

Vertical Fence

this version, although I have used maple, oak and even cherry, in the past. The edge guide base is made of MDF and its fence is cherry.

When assembling the mortising jig, glue the top to the riser and the riser to the base. When the glue dries, joint the front face of the jig to make sure it is all in one plane. Then joint the top surface to make sure that is square to the front face. Finally, cut the back edge of the top on the table saw to insure it is parallel to the front face. The pieces are thick enough so that you can joint them several times over the life of the jig. This can be quite helpful if the pieces seem to warp out of square over time (just make sure to remove the threaded inserts before jointing the face!).

Once the main part of the jig is together, you can drill for the various bolt holes, etc. The drawing has lots of dimensions all over it. None of these are especially critical. Make the pieces to suit the materials you have on hand. Your main concern is

to make sure the various faces of the jig are flat, square and parallel. The rabbet on the edge guide's fence should engage with the edge-guide rail on the back of the mortising jig.

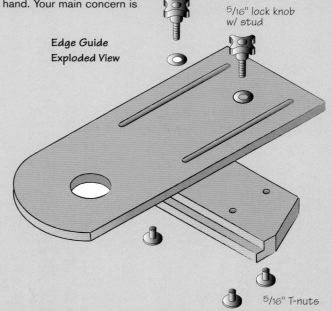

**Edge Guide
Exploded View**

5/16" lock knob
w/ stud

5/16" T-nuts

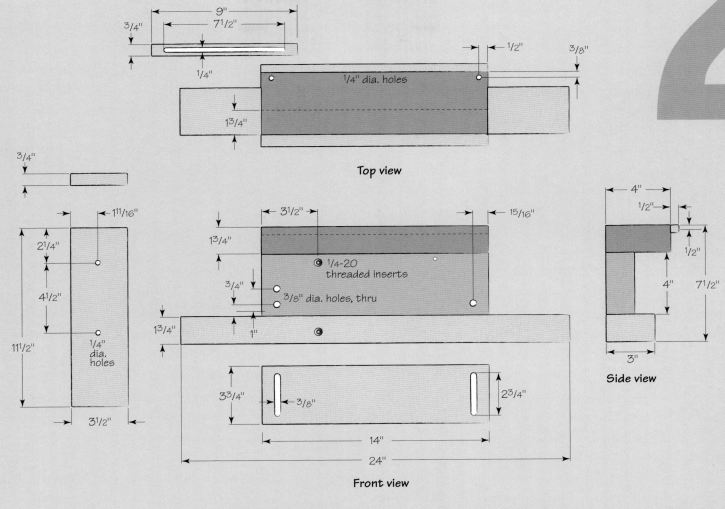

Top view

9"
7½"
¾"
¼"
½"
3/8"
¼" dia. holes
1¾"

Front view

3½"
15/16"
1¾"
1/4-20 threaded inserts
¾"
3/8" dia. holes, thru
1¾"
1"
3¾"
2¾"
3/8"
14"
24"

¾"
1 11/16"
2¼"
4½"
11½"
¼" dia. holes
3½"

4"
½"
½"
4"
7½"
3"

Side view

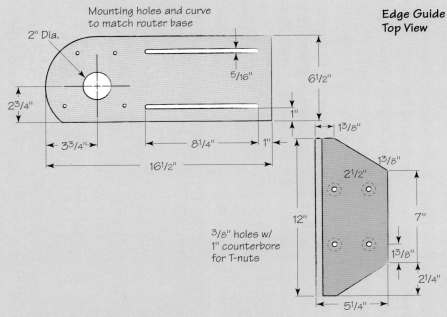

Mounting holes and curve to match router base

Edge Guide Top View

2" Dia.
2¾"
3¾"
5/16"
6½"
1"
8¼"
1"
16½"

3/8" holes w/ 1" counterbore for T-nuts

1 3/8"
2½"
1 3/8"
12"
7"
1 3/8"
2¼"
5¼"

kaleidoscope

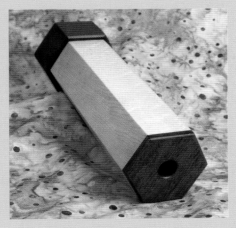

THE KALEIDOSCOPE has been intriguing folks since Sir David Brewster invented it in 1816. It seems to be one of those things that adds up to be much more than the sum of its parts — how can some bits of wood, a few pieces of glass and mirror and a handful of colorful baubles combine to make such an endless variety of intriguing patterns? Whether you make one of these "'scopes" as a gift, or keep it for your own pleasure, you can be sure it will give you many times your investment back in pure fun and enjoyment.

The kaleidoscope presented here is a pretty straightforward build. Two wooden, hexagonal cylinders combine to form the case for the inner workings. Making these tubes will give you a chance to play around with a birdsmouth bit — a bit specifically designed for cutting the joints for such an assembly.

The shorter cylinder contains what is called the object chamber, where you stash whatever you wish to appear inside the 'scope. Almost anything will work. Colored beads, bits of stained glass, and/or scraps of plastic are all commonly included. I've also seen really nice 'scopes that have used things you might not consider such as watch springs and gears and hardware store fasteners. The neat thing about this design is that you can experiment, loading all sorts of things into the chamber before committing to a particular mix.

The longer cylinder contains the mirror system, which creates the image, and the eyepiece that you look through. Feel free to play with the mirror configuration. Using mirrors of equal width produces the classic kaleidoscope image, but many others are possible. I made my kaleidoscope from birdseye maple and mahogany, but any wood(s) will work. Check your scrap bin and see what you have on hand.

KALEIDOSCOPE
inches (millimeters)

REFERENCE	QUANTITY	PART	STOCK	THICKNESS	(mm)	WIDTH	(mm)	LENGTH	(mm)
A	6	regular staves	hardwood	5/16	(8)	1 1/2	(38)	9 1/4	(235)
B	1	side stave	hardwood	5/16	(8)	1 11/16	(43)	14	(356)
C	1	end cap	hardwood	5/16	(8)	2 5/8	(67)	3	(76)

HARDWARE

1 clear glass single strength, 1/8" (3mm) x 4" (102mm) x 8" (203mm)

3 mirror (first surface), 1 1/2" (38mm) x 9 1/4" (235mm)

duct tape

packing peanuts

caulk

baubles, beads or other trinkets

BIT BOX

EAGLE AMERICA CATALOG NO.

6/12 sided birdsmouth, 1/2" shank, No. 190-2865

1/8" straight, 1/4" shank, No. 102-0202

1/8" roundover, 1/4" shank, No. 156-0202

45° chamfer, 1/2" shank, No. 152-0625

5/8" Forstner

2" Forstner

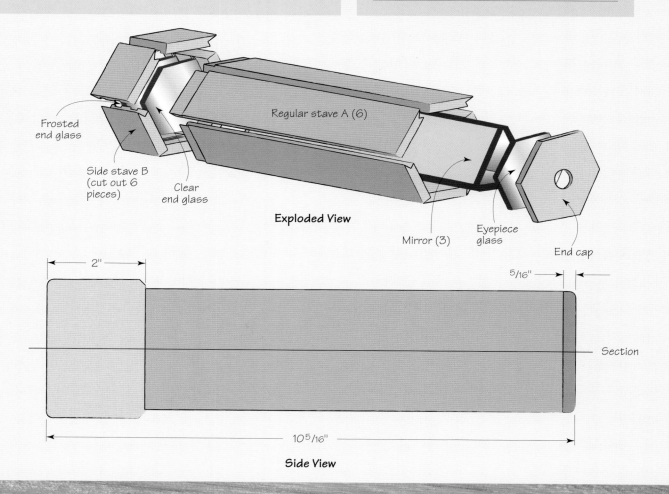

Frosted end glass

Side stave B (cut out 6 pieces)

Clear end glass

Regular stave A (6)

Exploded View

Mirror (3)

Eyepiece glass

End cap

2"

5/16"

Section

10 5/16"

Side View

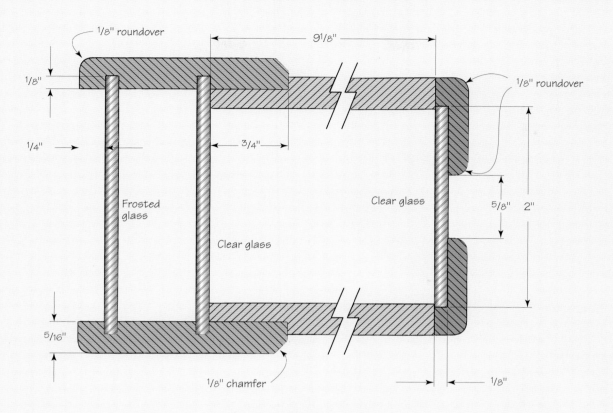

1/8" roundover

9 1/8"

1/8"

1/8" roundover

1/4"

3/4"

Frosted glass

Clear glass

5/8"   2"

Clear glass

Clear glass

5/16"

1/8" chamfer

1/8"

Cross Section

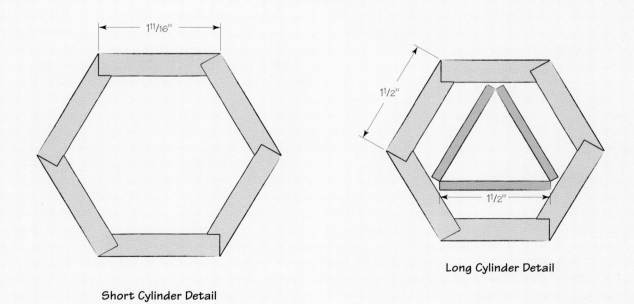

1 11/16"

1 1/2"

1 1/2"

Short Cylinder Detail

Long Cylinder Detail

STEP 1 Cut the six regular staves and the single wide stave to the thickness and widths given in the Materials List, but leave them an inch or so long for now. Chuck a 6/12 side birdsmouth bit in your table-mounted router. This is a big, honkin' bit and it may seem like overkill for such thin pieces, but it works just as well for thin stock as it does for thicker material. Adjust the bit height so its point is centered on the staves.

STEP 2 Bury the bit behind the face of your regular fence. Clamp a sacrificial fence to the front of the regular fence. Turn the router on and carefully move the fence assembly backwards, allowing the bit to cut through the sacrificial fence. Cut slightly further than you think you might need, then pull the fence forward so the bit is no longer touching the sacrificial fence.

STEP 3 Fine tune the fence position so that the bit leaves a slight ($1/32$") flat on the staves where they contact the fence. Cut one edge of each stave.

STEP 4 Apply glue to the birdsmouth cuts and put the regular staves together into a hexagon. After a lot of fumbling with the pieces, I found the easiest way to get them together was to stand them on end. Once you have all six staves together, apply rubber bands to serve as clamps. (Note, try to apply the pressure around the hexagon evenly. If you push too hard on one side without an equal force on the opposite side, you are likely to collapse the whole mess.)

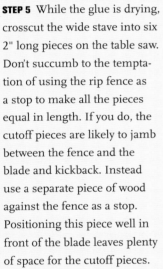

STEP 5 While the glue is drying, crosscut the wide stave into six 2" long pieces on the table saw. Don't succumb to the temptation of using the rip fence as a stop to make all the pieces equal in length. If you do, the cutoff pieces are likely to jamb between the fence and the blade and kickback. Instead use a separate piece of wood against the fence as a stop. Positioning this piece well in front of the blade leaves plenty of space for the cutoff pieces.

STEP 6 Once the glue is thoroughly dry, crosscut the ends of the hexagon to make sure the ends are flush and the entire piece is the right length.

STEP 7 Chuck a $1/8$" straight bit in your table-mounted router and adjust it to make a $1/8$" deep cut. Adjust the fence so it is $1/4$" away from the bit and rout dados across the six short staves. Use a push block to help control the pieces.

STEP 8 Put the short staves together to form a hexagon and slip a rubber band around the pieces to hold them together. Trace around the inside of the assembly twice to make patterns for the two glass pieces you'll be cutting. One piece will fit into the dadoes you just routed, the other must fit inside the shorter hexagon. On one of the tracings, lay out an additional set of lines $3/32$" outside the original lines to make the pattern for the larger piece. Cut a piece of glass to match the width (the distance between two opposing flats) of one of the patterns. Place this piece right on top of the pattern. Using a straightedge to help guide your cutter, make the angled cuts to complete the hexagon. Repeat the process using the second pattern.

Cutting Glass

Cutting glass is sort of a misnomer. The process is more of a controlled break. To make a "cut" you first score the surface of the glass to indicate where you would like the material to separate, then you snap the glass along this line. While the process is not terribly difficult, it does require a little practice.

Like most crafts, glasswork has its own special set of tools. One of the most basic is the glass cutter — a wand with a tiny wheel at one end that is hard enough to make a score mark or "run" across the glass's surface. Most hardware stores carry a basic cutter like the red one in the photo. These work quite well, especially for straight cuts. The other cutter in the photo is a more expensive model (available through stained glass suppliers). It features a pivoting head holding the wheel and a reservoir for lubricant. If you cut a lot of glass, and/or need to make curved cuts, the added expense is well worth it.

For a straight cut, position a straightedge along your line. If you're cutting a specific shape, make a paper pattern that you can work on top of. Or, you can measure and mark the glass with a grease pencil. (Note: unlike using a marking knife, you'll need to place the straightedge slightly to one side of the line to accommodate the thickness of the cutter.)

Before touching the cutter to the glass, you must lubricate it. Glass is so hard that it will ruin the cutter's wheel if you use it dry. There are several ways to apply lubrication. Many professional glass cutters keep a can of kerosene on their cutting table and dip their cutter before each cut. You can also squirt a little lubricant right on the glass at the start of each cut. Again, kerosene works well, but lately I've been using WD-40 as I almost always have some on hand. Also, my fancy cutter has a reservoir in the handle that I keep filled with WD-40. As I start a run, pushing down on the handle releases a squirt of oil to do the job.

To make a run, guide your cutter along the straightedge. Use firm, but not hard, pressure. The cutter should make a slight hissing sound as it scores the surface. Try to make the whole run in a single pass. Multiple passes tend to "confuse" the glass, giving it more than one direction it can snap, resulting in a lesser cut. Pay particular attention at the start and end of the run. If the run doesn't reach the edges of the glass, the break tends to wander off your line.

After making the run, snap the glass as soon as possible while the cut is still "hot". If you wait, the glass is less likely to snap where you want it to. For large pieces of glass, you can often snap them simply by flexing the piece towards the run. For smaller pieces, try slipping a pencil or dowel under the run and pressing down on either side. You can also purchase various running pliers with convex/concave jaws made for just this purpose. (Note: trying to snap off a narrow sliver of glass, anything less than about 1/2" wide, is very difficult. If you have to trim a little bit off a piece, you may be better off to re-cut the whole thing.)

9

10

STEP 9 Frost the larger of the two hexagonal pieces of glass (see Frosting Your Own Glass below). Slip the glass in the dados and reassemble the short hexagonal cylinder to check its fit. Once you are satisfied, apply glue to the joints and clamp the cylinder together with rubber bands.

STEP 10 Before cutting the end cap to size, make sure it will cover the end of the longer hexagonal cylinder if you cut it to the sizes listed. Find the center by drawing diagonals across the piece. Drill a $5/8"$ hole through the piece at the center. Mount a $1/8"$ roundover bit in your table-mounted router. Start the router and carefully set the end cap over the bit. Run the cap around the bit's bearing to round over the edges of the eye hole. Lift the piece off the bit before you shut down the router.

Frosting Your Own Glass

You can purchase glass that is pre-frosted, but it is not nearly as inexpensive or readily available as clear. (Many glass shops may even give you the few small pieces you need to make this kaleidoscope.) To frost glass on you own, you have a couple options. If you have access to a sand blaster, you can easily frost the pieces you need in a few short minutes. Or, you can sand the glass with a random orbit sander. Use double-sided tape to hold the glass to your bench and go over it with a medium-grit paper. Be very careful not to bump the edge of the glass with the edge of the disc or you may dislodge it and send it flying — I learned this one the hard way! Sand both sides of the glass for best results.

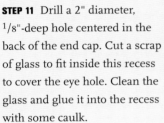

11

12

13

STEP 11 Drill a 2" diameter, 1/8"-deep hole centered in the back of the end cap. Cut a scrap of glass to fit inside this recess to cover the eye hole. Clean the glass and glue it into the recess with some caulk.

STEP 12 Rabbet the end of the longer cylinder so it will fit in the shorter cylinder. Chuck a 1-inch straight bit in your table-mounted router. Adjust it to make a cut slightly less than 1/8" deep. Place the fence over the bit, leaving 3/4" of the bit exposed. Push the cylinder along the fence with a guide block to make the cuts. Cut all six sides. Check the fit of the pieces. Raise the bit slightly and re-cut if necessary.

STEP 13 Center the end cap on the non-rabbeted end of the longer cylinder and glue it in place. I know you're gluing to end grain, but the piece will be under no stress, so it should be fine. If you are worried about the joint failing, drill through the end cap and add 1/8" diameter reinforcing dowels after the glue dries. Cut and sand the edges of the end cap flush with the sides of the cylinder.

STEP 14 Chuck a 1/8" roundover bit in your table-mounted router and round over the corners of the shorter cylinder on the outside (glass) end. Also round over the edges of the end cap on the longer cylinder. Switch to a chamfer bit and chamfer the corners on the open end of the shorter cylinder.

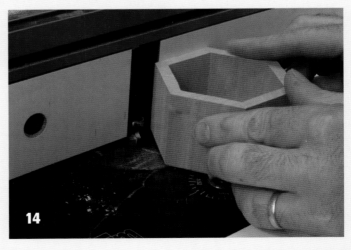

14

STEP 15 Clean your bench top thoroughly to keep the dust to a minimum. Cut the mirrors to the size specified. Stretch out two strips of duct tape sticky side up on your bench. (I used double-sided tape on the bench to help hold the duct tape in place.) Place the mirror on the duct tape starting near one end and spacing the pieces about 1/8" apart. Clean the mirrors.

STEP 16 Roll the mirrors up into a triangle and wrap the remaining duct tape around them to hold everything together. Peer through the middle of the triangle to check for gaps. Stretch short lengths of duct tape around the corners to improve the way the mirrors fit. (Note: Using mirrors of equal width produces the classic, equilateral triangle pattern inside the 'scope. Don't feel limited by this; varying the width of the mirrors in relationship to each other can produce many stunning effects. Experiment if you are feeling adventurous.)

15

16

Mirrors for Kaleidoscopes

The mirrored surface of most mirrors is behind the glass. This way the glass protects the fragile silvered surface from scratches. This is a good thing for a household mirror, but not the best for a kaleidoscope. In a kaleidoscope, having the glass in front of the mirror degrades the quality of the reflection somewhat. Instead, try to find "first surface" mirror (available from stained glass suppliers and many other glass shops). With first surface mirror, the reflective coating is on the surface of the glass. It's more fragile, but inside a kaleidoscope, this isn't really important. It does, however, make for much crisper reflections. (Note: When cutting first surface mirror, be sure to make your runs on the non-silvered side.)

3

STEP 17 After one final check for dust, slide the mirror assembly into the cylinder. Use Styrofoam packing peanuts to center the mirrors and keep them from rattling around.

STEP 18 When you are sure all is well with the mirrors, caulk the smaller, clear hexagonal glass piece over the open end of the longer cylinder, sealing the mirrors inside. Be sure to clean the inside surface of the glass.

STEP 19 Experiment with the objects you put in the object chamber. Bits of stained glass, colored beads, almost anything with an interesting color and/or shape make for good candidates. Play with the quantity as well as the mix of objects until you like what you see through the eye hole.

STEP 20 If you are going to stain parts of the kaleidoscope, do it before final assembly. Tape off the glass to make clean up easier. Apply the stain and allow it to dry. Glue the two cylinders together before applying the final finish. I used a dark red mahogany stain on the darker parts on the piece in the photos, then finished the whole 'scope with several coats of Deft Spray Lacquer. I like using lacquer on maple because it doesn't tend to make it too yellow.

CD shelf

IF STEVE JOBS CONTINUES on his current path with the iPod, the audio CD may go the way of the LP record and the dodo bird. But for now, most of us still rely on these ubiquitous plastic discs for our daily tunes. As with any item that we own, storage almost immediately becomes an issue — what can we do with these things when they are not in use so that they don't get lost, are protected, and yet remain easily accessible?

Those three things were in my mind as I designed this CD storage shelf. I wanted to make a storage system that would corral and organize my music collection without restricting access. It also had to look good in the process. And, since I was designing the unit to include in this book, it had to rely primarily on the router for construction. I think you'll see it succeeds on all these fronts.

Construction revolves around some router fundamentals — cutting accurate dadoes and rabbets. You'll also have the opportunity to do some pattern routing as you cut the sides to shape. Actually, that is one of the neater tricks you'll learn here. Rather than going through the hassle of creating a pattern just to make the two side pieces, I made up one of the side pieces first, then used it as a pattern for the second. A little bit of profile routing completes the show.

The shelf shown here is made from luan mahogany and hard maple, a combination I like a lot. I've also made a shelf similar to this one for my older daughter and have painted (and repainted) the sides to suit her current favorite color. Having the sides screwed (not glued) to the shelves really facilitates her redecorating whims.

CD SHELF
inches (millimeters)

REFERENCE	QUANTITY	PART	STOCK	THICKNESS	(mm)	WIDTH	(mm)	LENGTH	(mm)
A	2	sides	hardwood	$5/8$	(16)	8	(203)	$32^{5/8}$	(829)
B	3	shelves	hardwood	$3/4$	(19)	7	(178)	22	(559)
C	1	top cross piece	hardwood	$5/8$	(16)	$2^{1/4}$	(57)	$21^{3/4}$	(552)
D	3	narrow cross pieces	hardwood	$5/8$	(16)	$1^{1/2}$	(38)	$21^{3/4}$	(552)

HARDWARE

16   No. 8 x $2^{1/2}$" (65mm)
flathead wood screws

16   No. 8 finishing washers

BIT BOX

EAGLE AMERICA CATALOG NO.

$3/4$" straight, $1/2$" shank, No. 102-1225

1" pattern, $1/2$" shank, No. 102-1625B

$3/8$" roundover, $1/2$" shank, No. 156-0605

$1/4$" roundover, $1/2$" shank, No. 156-0405

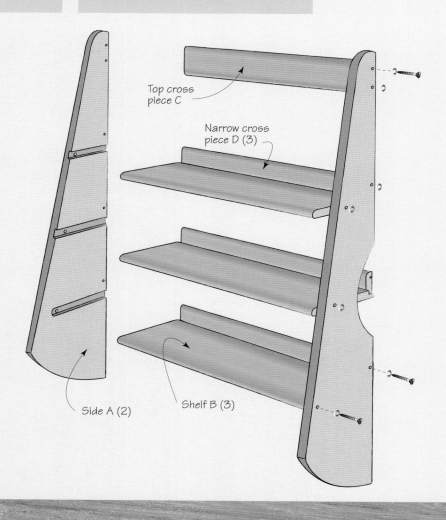

Top cross piece C

Narrow cross piece D (3)

Side A (2)

Shelf B (3)

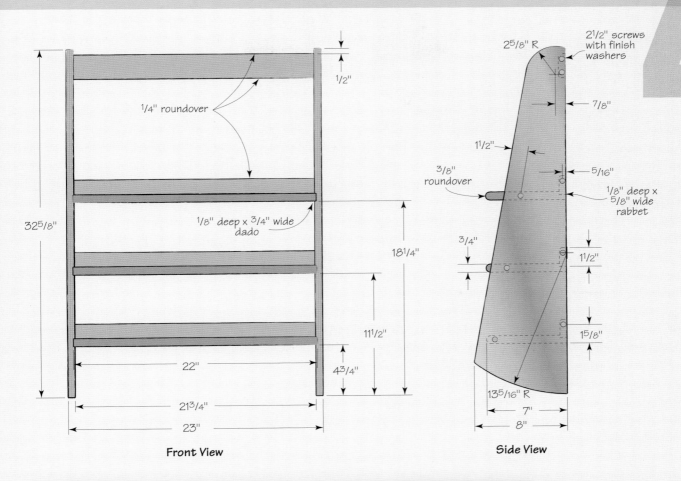

1/4" roundover

32⁵/8"

1/2"

1/8" deep x 3/4" wide dado

18¹/4"

11¹/2"

22"

4³/4"

21³/4"

23"

Front View

2⁵/8" R

2¹/2" screws with finish washers

7/8"

1¹/2"

3/8" roundover

5/16"

1/8" deep x 5/8" wide rabbet

3/4"

1¹/2"

1⁵/8"

13⁵/16" R

7"

8"

Side View

STEP 1 Cut the sides to size. Clamp them together side by side. This simplifies layout, and it elevates the pieces off the surface of your bench which makes it easier to clamp the router guide in place. Draw lines across the sides to locate the bottom of each shelf as shown in the Front View.

STEP 2 Cut the dados for the shelves with a 3/4" straight bit in your plunge router, using a straightedge as a guide. (See Enhanced Straightedges on page 59.) To cut each dado, clamp the straightedge across the sides with its edge aligned with the layout line. (Note: In this instance, the straightedge should be placed on the side of the line towards the bottom end of the sides.) Double-check to make sure the straightedge is square to the edges of the sides. Set the depth of cut to 1/8". Rout the dado from left to right. Cut the dados for the top two shelves all the way across both sides. (Note: To help keep the router from tipping, you can clamp an outrigger to the sides about 2" away from the straightedge.)

STEP 3 The dado for the bottom shelf stops 1" from the outside (front) edge of both sides. Clamp the straightedge in place as before. (You may need to move the clamp holding the sides together.) Mark the sides where you want the dado to start and stop. Clamp stops to the straightedge to prevent the router from traveling past these points. Rout the dado from left to right, plunging the bit into the shelf to start and lifting it again when the router touches the right-hand stop.

STEP 4 Lay out the taper and the curves on the left-hand side as shown in the Side View.

STEP 5 Cut the side roughly to shape on the band saw or with a saber saw. Straighten the long tapered edge with a block plane. Then sand the curves true.

6A

6B

STEP 6 Once you are satisfied with the shape of the left side, use it as a pattern to rout the right side to shape. Trace the shape onto the second side and rough-cut it to remove most of the waste. Fasten the two pieces together with double-sided tape, being careful to align them along their back edges. Also check to make sure the dadoes match up. Chuck a pattern-cutting bit in your table-mounted router and adjust its height so the guide bearing rides along the edge of the first side without getting hung up in the dadoes. Rout the right side starting at the wide end of the taper and moving the pieces from right to left so you are cutting with the grain. Slow down as you round the curve at the top to minimize tearout as the bit exits the cut.

Pattern Routing

When pattern routing, you can often use either a flush-trim bit (right), or a pattern-cutting bit (left). The difference is mainly where the pattern goes. With a pattern-cutting bit, the guide bearing is mounted on the shank end of the bit. So the pattern needs to be mounted on the router side of the work piece – on a router table, this puts it underneath, with a handheld router, it goes on top. The opposite is true of a flushtrim bit. Depending on what you are doing, the two bits are practically interchangeable with one caveat: Flush-trim bits tend to be fairly slender (typically $1/2$" in diameter) and therefore will tend to vibrate more than pattern-cutting bits.

STEP 7 Pop the pieces apart and tape them together again, this time with their outside faces together. Rout the curve at the bottom of the side. By swapping the pieces around, you'll have set up to make the curved cut with the grain, greatly reducing the possibility of tear-out.

STEP 8 Cut the shelves to size. Chuck a 3/8" roundover bit in your table-mounted router. Adjust the fence so it is tangent to the guide bearing. Round over the top and bottom front edges of all three shelves, creating a bullnose profile.

STEP 9 Chuck a 3/4" straight bit in your table-mounted router and set it to make a 1/8" deep cut. Position the fence so the bit will make a 5/8"-wide cut. Cut a rabbet on the back edge of all three shelves. (Note: Run the pieces with their good side down as the rabbet should face up.)

STEP 10 Cut the cross pieces to the listed width and thickness, but leave them a little long for now. Chuck a $1/4$" roundover bit in your table-mounted router. Round over one edge on each of the narrow cross pieces, and two edges of the wide cross piece.

STEP 11 Sand all the pieces. Fit the shelves in the dadoes in the sides and clamp the unit together. Cut the cross pieces to a snug fit in between the sides. Glue the narrow cross pieces in the rabbets cut in the shelves. You may need to do this in two stages — first the top and bottom shelves, then the middle one to keep the clamps from interfering with each other.

STEP 12 Drill $3/16$" holes through the sides as shown in the Side View. Use a fence on the drill press to help position the holes properly. Place the holes $1^{1}/2$" in from the front edge and $5/16$" in from the back.

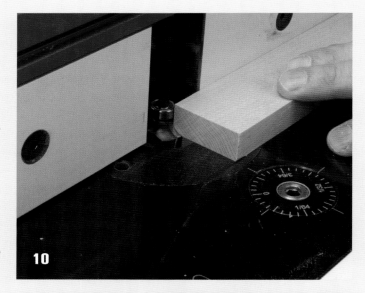

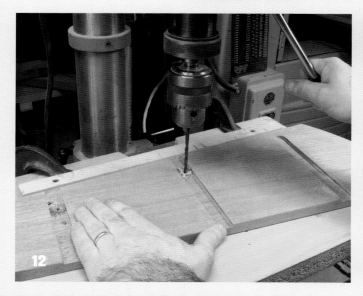

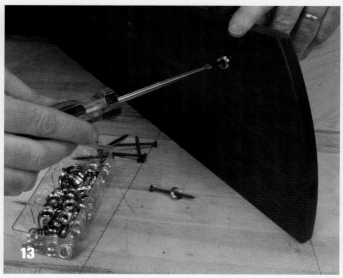

STEP 13 Finish all the pieces while they are apart. I used a red mahogany stain to darken the sides, then finished everything with a clear, water-based top coat. I like using water-based finishes on maple because they don't make it as yellow as oil-based finished do. When you are ready, assemble the unit and drill pilot holes for the screws into the ends of the shelves and cross pieces. Fasten the pieces together with $2^{1}/2$" screws and finish washers. To hang the shelf, I drive a pair of screws through one of the cross pieces into the wall studs. I use finish washers on the mounting screws as I did on the sides.

4

Enhanced Straightedges

Using a straightedge to guide a router is just about the oldest trick in the book. You slap it on your work, clamp it down and run your router along it to produce a nice straight cut. The only problem is positioning it to begin with. Because the router bit is some distance away from the actual straightedge, you have to do some pretty accurate measuring to get it in the right place. Rather than do this for each cut I want to make, I use what I've come to call an "enhanced straightedge."

An enhanced straightedge consists of a straightedge (typically a nice straight piece of 4/4 scrap about 2^1/$_2$" wide) with an added base screwed to it.

I usually make the base from a 5"-wide piece of ^{1}/$_4$" hardboard (Masonite) or MDF. The length varies depending on the application – 48" long makes a good general purpose model.

Start by jointing and cutting the straightedge so it is straight and true. Screw the base piece to the underside of the straightedge so one edge of the base is flush with one edge of the straightedge. Space the screws about 6" apart. Clamp the straightedge to your bench with the free side of the base hanging out over the edge. Chuck whatever bit you intend to use in your router. Run the router along the straightedge, trimming the base in the process.

This will create an enhanced straightedge that is specific to that combination of router and bit. I write this information on the straightedge so it is easy to find. As a final step, run the enhanced straightedge through the table saw, guiding it past the blade with the newly routed edge against the fence. Trim the outside edge to make sure both long edges are parallel. You never know when this might prove handy.

To use the enhanced straightedge, simply draw a line on your workpiece where you plan to cut. Clamp the straightedge in place with the edge of the base aligned with the line and rout away.

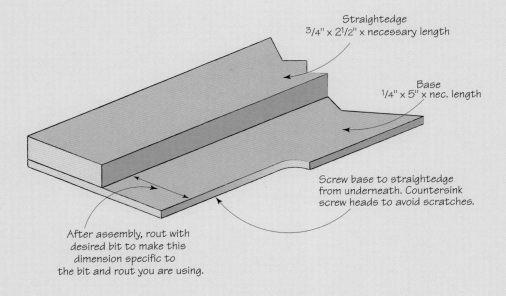

Straightedge
3/4" x 2^1/$_2$" x necessary length

Base
1/4" x 5" x nec. length

Screw base to straightedge from underneath. Countersink screw heads to avoid scratches.

After assembly, rout with desired bit to make this dimension specific to the bit and rout you are using.

tilt-top table

WHEN I WAS IN HIGH SCHOOL, the second piece of furniture I made was a small, Queen Anne style, tilt-top table. The design came from a book of plans for simple colonial furniture written by a fellow named Franklin H. Gottshall. As I recall, the book had excellent drawings but not much in the way of description as to how to actually build the piece. I find this a little serendipitous because I now teach at the same high school where Mr. Gottshall spent much of his career.

When I started designing pieces for this book, I decided to revisit the tilt-top table design and put a contemporary spin on it. The original tilt-top tables were often used as candle stands or tea tables. The tilting feature meant the table could be kept out of the way against a wall or in a corner until it was needed. I kept that aspect of the design, while stripping away much of the ornamentation of the older pieces.

The base is a truncated pyramid with compound miter joints at the corners. My intention was to build a router table with a tilting top to cut the miters, but it didn't work out too well. However, I've included a photo and some notes about construction. I think it can be made to work with a little tinkering and I invite you to try. I think there are some neat possibilities for different profiles that can be made by tilting the workpiece in relationship to some of the standard bits.

The tabletop is a circle, cut with a trammel jig. It does indeed tilt, exposing a smaller table surface that might serve as a stage for a rose in a bud vase or a candle.

TILT-TOP TABLE
inches (millimeters)

REFERENCE	QUANTITY	PART	STOCK	THICKNESS	(mm)	WIDTH	(mm)	LENGTH	(mm)
A	4	sides	hardwood	3/4	(19)	11	(279)	22 3/4	(578)
B	1	top	hardwood	3/4	(19)	18	(457)	18	(457)
C	1	sub top	hardwood	3/4	(19)	7	(178)	7	(178)
D	2	ribs	hardwood	5/8	(16)	1 1/4	(32)	9 1/2	(241)
E	1	mounting block	hardwood	3/4	(19)	1	(25)	1	(25)
F	2	pivot dowels	hardwood			3/8 D	(10)	1 1/2	(38)
G	2	locking dowels	hardwood			3/8 D	(10)	2	(51)
H	2	stops	hardwood			3/8 D	(10)	1 1/8	(29)
J	2	plugs	hardwood			3/8 D	(10)		
K	1	template	hardwood	3/4	(19)	12	(305)	22 13/16	(579)

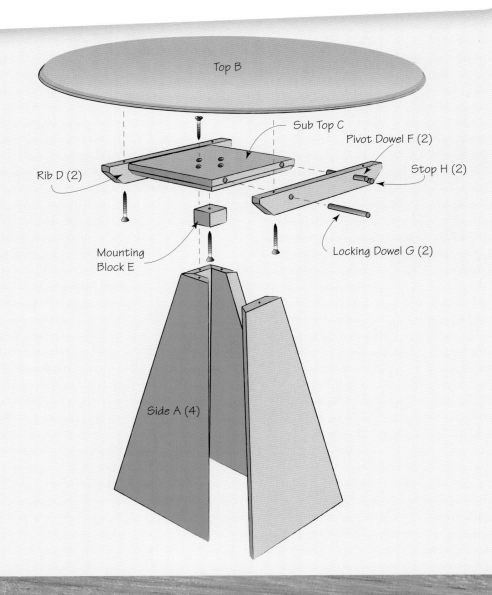

Top B

Sub Top C

Pivot Dowel F (2)

Rib D (2)

Stop H (2)

Locking Dowel G (2)

Mounting Block E

Side A (4)

BIT BOX

EAGLE AMERICA CATALOG NO.

3/4" straight, 1/2" shank, No. 102-1225

1" pattern, 1/2" shank, No. 102-1625B

1/2" spiral downcut, 1/2" shank, No. 106-0895

6/12 sided birdsmouth, 1/2" shank, No. 190-2865

1/4" roundover, 1/2" shank, No. 156-0405

3/8" spiral upcut, 1/2" shank, No. 106-0615

45° chamfer, 1/2" shank, No. 152-0625

3/8" roundover, 1/2" shank, No. 156-0605

3/8" plug cutter

HARDWARE

4   No. 8 x 1 3/4" (45mm) brass flathead screws

4   No. 8 x 2 1/2" (65mm) flathead screws

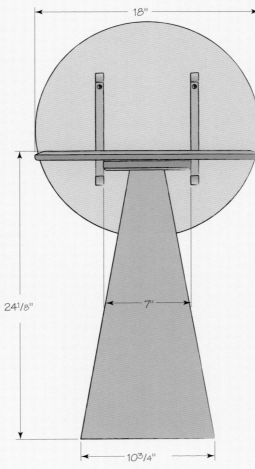

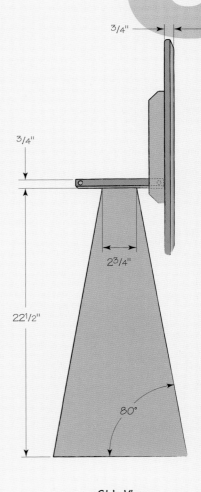

Front View

Side View

STEP 1 Cut a piece of MDF to serve as a template for the sides of the base. Lay out a center line along its length. Carefully lay out the angled sides as shown in the Template Detail on page 64.

Compound Miters

Because the base tilts in towards its top, the miter angle between the pieces isn't 45° as you might expect. Nor do the sides taper exactly 10° which is what shows on the drawing. Instead, the miter angle is 44 1/4° and the taper is 80 1/4°. These are subtle distinctions for sure, but enough to make the difference between joints that go together well and those that don't. The following chart gives the angles necessary for other compound miters.

TILT	MITER ANGLE	TAPER
5°	44 3/4°	85°
10°	44 1/4°	80 1/4°
15°	43 1/4°	75 1/2°
20°	41 3/4°	71 1/4°
25°	40°	67°
30°	37 3/4°	63 1/2°
35°	35 1/4°	60 1/4°
40°	32 1/2°	57 1/4°
45°	30°	54 3/4°

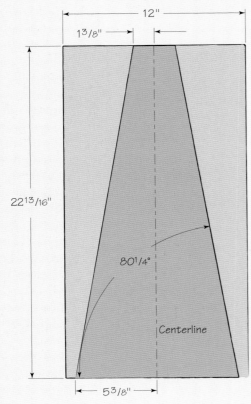

Tilt-Template Detail

12"

1 3/8"

22 13/16"

80 1/4°

Centerline

5 3/8"

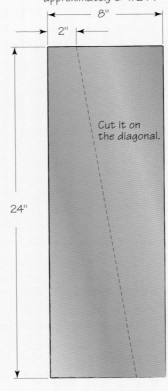

Start with a piece that is approximately 8" x 24".

8"

2"

24"

Cut it on the diagonal.

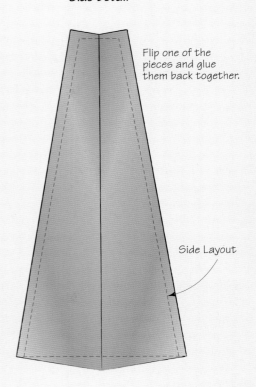

Side Detail

Flip one of the pieces and glue them back together.

Side Layout

STEP 2 Cut just outside the layout lines on the band saw. Then clamp a straight edge along one of the lines and rout the template to its final shape with a $^3/_4$" straight bit in a handheld router. Repeat the process with the second side of the template. Double-check to make sure the angles are correct.

STEP 3 Glue up pieces to make panels wide enough for the sides. To save material and arrange the grain to compliment the shape of the pieces, consider cutting your material diagonally as shown in the Side Detail. I did this with my table and was pleased with the end result. Once you have the sides ready, trace the outline of the template onto them and cut close to the line on the band saw. Screw the template to the back of each side in turn.

STEP 4 Chuck a pattern bit in your table-mounted router and rout the sides to shape. Another advantage of gluing the panels on a diagonal is that you'll be cutting both sides more or less with the grain in this operation.

STEP 5 Tilt the blade on your table saw to an 80° angle (10° from vertical). Cut the bottom of each side off at this angle. Guide the pieces through the cut using a miter gauge with an auxiliary fence. You'll need to tilt the blade to compensate for the taper of the side. Clamp a stop to the fence to control the length of the pieces. After cutting the bottoms of the pieces, repeat the process to cut the tops at the same angle.

STEP 6 Tilt the fence on your jointer to cut a $44^1/_4$° angle. Make test cuts to be sure you have the setting correct.

STEP 7 Joint the miter angle onto both tapered edges of each side piece. Run the inside face of each piece against the fence. Count the number of passes it takes to complete the first miter and then run all the other edges that same number of times. This should keep all four pieces the same width.

STEP 8 After trying several different ways to glue up miter joints, I have come to the conclusion that the best way to do it is to glue clamp blocks right to the pieces you want to join. Then, once the glue sets, you'll be able to apply pressure directly across the joint without having to worry about the pieces slipping. Cut one side of the clamp blocks at a 45° angle (close enough to $44\frac{1}{4}$°) and glue them near the edges of the sides as shown. No need to overdo the glue — just put some in three or four places along the length of the pieces. Clamp things together until the glue dries.

STEP 9 Apply glue to the miter faces and glue the four sides together. (Note: If, after all your careful machine work, the four corners don't want to fit nicely, just glue up two opposing corners. Then, after the glue is dry, you can fine tune the fit of the two remaining corners with a hand plane.)

STEP 10 Glue together enough pieces to make a panel wide enough for the top. Locate its center on the underside by drawing diagonals from corner to corner. Lay out an 18"-diameter circle and cut the top roughly to shape on the band saw. Drill a $\frac{5}{16}$"-diameter hole at the center point. Be careful not to drill all the way through the top. Attach a small trammel (see Small Trammel on facing page) to the base of your router. Rout the top round with a $\frac{1}{2}$" spiral down-cut bit. Down-cut bits are nice because they throw the debris down, away from the cut. They also leave a smooth cut on the top surface, although in this situation it doesn't matter as the top is upside down.

5

Small Trammel

This trammel jig will allow you to cut circles from 2 to 30 inches in diameter. Combined with the Large Trammel shown on page 100, the two jigs should cover most of your circle-cutting needs.

This jig is designed to be screwed to the base of a hand-held router. I prefer a plunge router as it allows me to start a circular cut with the bit out of contact of the workpiece. One of the next things I intend to design is a quick-mounting system for attaching such jigs to a router.

I made my trammel from a scrap of Baltic birch plywood with a hardwood slider. The pivot pin is a piece of steel cut from a 5/16" bolt. The clamp block is poplar. You'll notice the block in the photo doesn't quite match the drawing. When I first made the trammel, I went with a longer block and quickly discovered that it interfered with the router's handle. I fixed things by moving the location of the lock knob, but left the original block in place. I suggest you follow the drawing rather than the photo for this detail.

The slider fits in a T-groove cut in the underside of the jig. It is locked in place by tightening the knob. The knob is threaded through a T-nut and presses on a metal disc, which presses on the slider. I used a slug from an electric junction box for the metal plate, but a quarter would also work well. As with all jigs, vary the sizes of things to fit your needs.

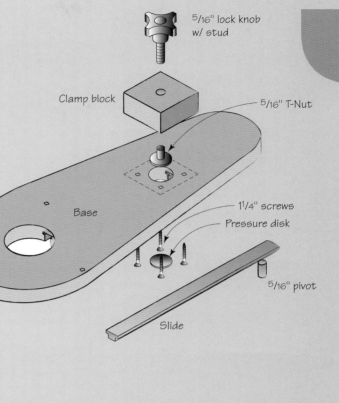

5/16" lock knob w/ stud

Clamp block

5/16" T-Nut

Base

1 1/4" screws

Pressure disk

5/16" pivot

Slide

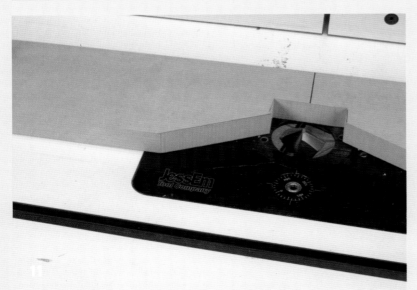

STEP 11 Chuck a 6/12 birdsmouth bit in your table-mounted router (see Misusing Bits, page 70) and adjust its height to about 3/8". Clamp a V-fence to your router table surrounding the bit. See V-fence on page 68 for a drawing of the fence's opening.

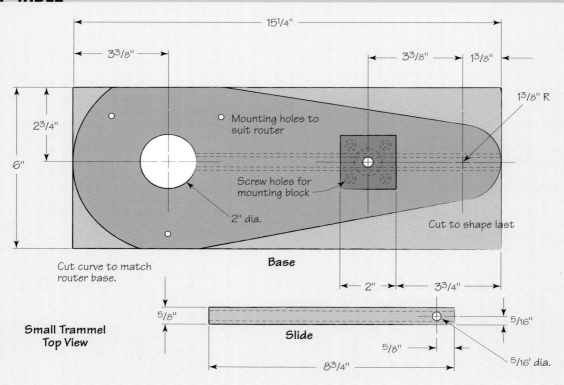

15¼"

3⅜"   3⅜"   1⅜"

2¾"

6"

1⅜" R

○ Mounting holes to suit router

Screw holes for mounting block

2" dia.

Cut to shape last

Base

Cut curve to match router base.

2"   3¾"

5/8"   5/16"

Small Trammel Top View

Slide

5/8"

5/16' dia.

8¾"

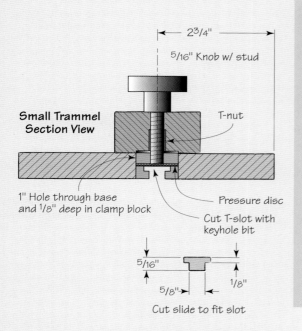

2¾"

5/16" Knob w/ stud

Small Trammel Section View

T-nut

1" Hole through base and ⅛" deep in clamp block

Pressure disc

Cut T-slot with keyhole bit

5/16"

⅛"

5/8"

Cut slide to fit slot

V-Fence

A V-fence is a handy device if you do much circular work. It allows you to guide a circular (or semi-circular) workpiece past a router bit without having to rely on a guide bearing. This opens up all sorts of possibilities for different profiles depending on the bits in your collection. Make the fence from a scrap of plywood or MDF. It should be long enough to span your router table from side to side.

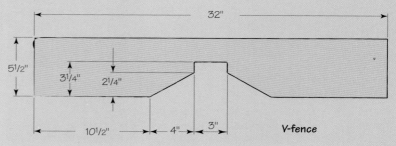

32"

5½"

3¼"

2¼"

V-fence

10½"   4"   3"

STEP 12 Set the tabletop on the router table topside down and adjust the fence so the edge of the top almost reaches the center of the bit. Readjust the bit height so the bit cuts about 5/16" off the top edge.

STEP 13 Start the router and pivot the top into the cut off of the left-hand corner of the V opening. Slowly turn the top counterclockwise to make the cut, keeping the top in contact with both sides of the fence at all times. (Don't worry if the top comes away from the fence at some point, just keep turning it until you recut the problem area.

12

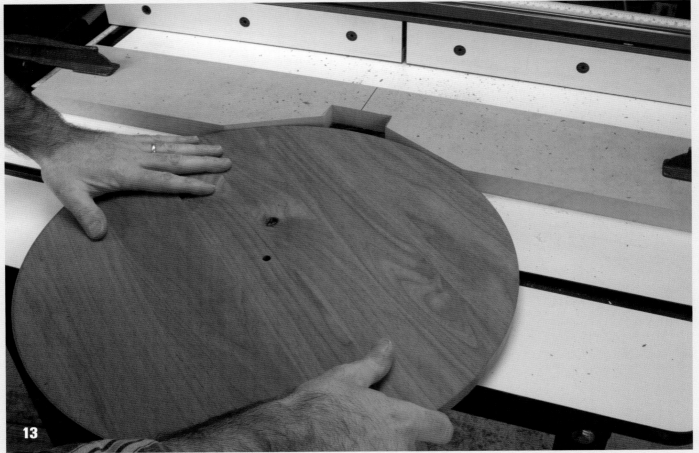

13

14

"Misusing" Bits

When I'm trying to decide on a profile for a design, I usually decide on the shape first, and then figure out how to create it. Oftentimes I'll look at my bit collection to see what bits I have that will give me something at least close to the profile I want. That way, I won't have to shell out money for yet another piece of tooling. In the case of this tilt-top table, I needed a bit that would cut a bevel around the edge of the top. I noticed that the top of my 6/12 birdsmouth bit had about the right angle, so I used it. The resulting bevel looks great, even though that profile isn't exactly what the manufacturer intended.

15

STEP 14 Swap the birdsmouth bit for a 1/4" roundover bit. Turn the top rightside up and roundover the bottom edge. Again, turn the piece counterclockwise to make the cut, while keeping the top in contact with the bit's bearing.

STEP 15 Cut the sub top to size. Lay out the positions of the pivot holes on the ends of the sub top as shown in the Sub Top Detail. Install the vertical fence on your mortising jig and clamp the top to the jig with the grain running vertically.

Chuck a 3/8" spiral upcut bit in your plunge router and carefully center it across the thickness of the piece, using an edge guide to control the router's position. Use the stops on the jig to control the router's lateral movement and to position the

bit over the hole layout. Plunge the hole to a depth of 1". Pivot the sub top and plunge a hole on the second end. Flip the piece over so the opposite face is against the fence and plunge the second hole in each end.

16

STEP 16 Chuck a 45° chamfer bit in your table-mounted router and adjust it to make a cut that stops a little shy of the holes you just routed. Make the cuts by running the pieces along the fence from left to right.

STEP 17 Switch the chamfer bit for a 3/8" roundover bit. Round over one of the long grain edges (parallel to the holes) of the sub top. This is the back edge of the sub top.

17

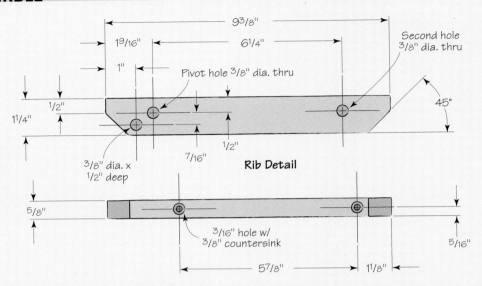

Rib Detail

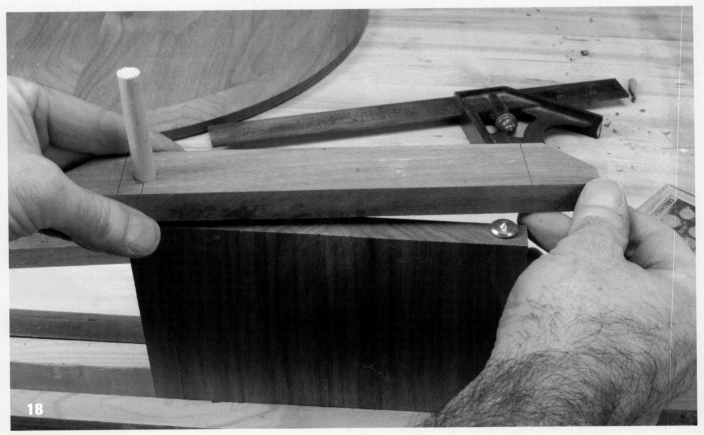

18

STEP 18 Cut the ribs to the size indicated and cut off the two lower corners at 45° as shown in the Rib Detail. Drill the $3/8$" pivot hole in one end of each rib as shown. Slip a dowel through the hole and into the corresponding hole in the sub top. Put a dowel center in the other hole in the sub top. Align the rib so it is parallel to the sub top and mark the location of the second hole by pressing the rib down onto the dowel center. Repeat with the second rib on the opposite end of the sub top. Drill the marked holes through both ribs. Drill the stop holes $1/2$" deep as indicated in the drawing.

19

STEP 19 Drill four $^3/16$" mounting holes in the sub top as shown in the Sub Top Detail. Counterbore these holes for $^3/8$" plugs from the top side. Cut the mounting block to be a snug fit in the opening in the top of the base. Glue and screw it to the center of the subbase, making sure to keep it square to the edges of the larger piece.

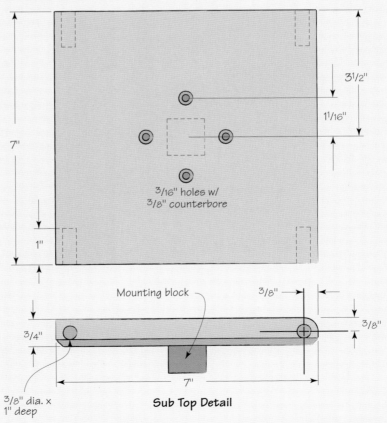

$3^1/2$"

$1^1/16$"

7"

3/16" holes w/
3/8" counterbore

1"

Mounting block

3/8"

3/8"

3/4"

7"

3/8" dia. x
1" deep

Sub Top Detail

Resizing Dowels

If you need to trim a dowel to fit in a hole, one of the easiest ways is to chuck it into an electric drill and sand it to the right diameter. If you want to make the dowels removable, as is the case with the tilt-top table, you can sand the dowels to a slight taper. This will make them easy to insert into their holes, and tight when they are fully seated.

STEP 20 Drill and countersink $^3/_{16}$" clearance holes for the mounting screws through the ribs. Slide temporary $^3/_8$" dowels through the holes in the ribs and into the holes in the sub top. Center the assembly on the top. Screw it in place with brass $2^3/_4$" flathead wood screws. (Note: When screwing things together with brass screws, I always purchase a few steel screws of the same size. Then, when it comes time to cut the threads for the first time, I use the steel screws rubbed with a little wax. Going this route makes twisting the head off of brass screws much less likely.)

STEP 21 Unscrew one of the ribs so you can take the sub top off and position it on top of the base. Drill pilot holes and screw the sub base to the base with $2^1/_2$" screws. Then, plug the holes.

STEP 22 Finish the pieces before adding the top to the base. When you are ready, slide matching hardwood dowels into the pivot holes. Before you drive them in the last little bit, wipe on a little glue, then tap them home. Also, glue the stops in the holes drilled in the ribs. Finally, carve a notch or two around the ends of the locking dowels and insert them in their holes — they should fit snugly, but not so tight that you can't pull them back out. The notches are to provide a little grip for your fingers.

An Idea in Need of Perfecting

The tilt-top router table is an idea worth perfecting. I added a tilting top to a small, benchtop router table that I use when I do demonstrations away from my shop. You can get a look at the basic idea in the photo. There are two slotted blocks that are mounted to the underside of the router table at either side. These are attached using hanger bolts that are screwed into the underside of the table. The bolts go through the slots and are secured with knobs. The slots allow you to move the sliding table back and forth in relationship to the bit. Quadrants with curved slots attach the actual tilting tabletop to the slotted blocks. While this setup didn't produce the kind of accuracy I needed to cut perfect compound miters, it did produce some interesting profiles. I've included it here in case some of you are looking for something interesting to tinker with. Let me know what you come up with.

folding screen

IF YOU'RE LOOKING for a project that is a little unusual but still quite practical, consider this folding screen. Stashed in the corner of a room, it makes a great backdrop for your favorite chair, but it is ready for more demanding work in an instant. When I was growing up, my parents had such a screen that they broke out each year on Christmas morning to shield my young eyes from the wonders of the tree until after breakfast.

Replace one of the wooden panels with a mirror, and you'll have a dynamite dressing screen. Or better yet, replace all three panels with mirror and you'll have a screen fit for the most demanding fashion connoisseur. If you go this route, get $1/8"$ mirror to go in the frame and back it with $1/8"$ plywood to protect the backside of the mirror from scratches.

From a construction standpoint, the screen frames offer several challenges. The joinery is cut with a set of matched cope-and-stick router bits. Once you have them set up, they'll cut tight-fitting joints all day — provided you run the pieces past them with care. Featherboards are a must with this operation, particularly when dealing with pieces as long as the ones you'll use for the frame stiles.

The rails have a stepped shape along their outside edges. This is cut with a pattern bit and a sandwich template. A sandwich template is two sided so you can flip the whole thing over partway through the cut and avoid having to make any part of the cut against the grain. Even if you don't build the screen, it's worth taking a look at how this kind of template goes together — it can be quite handy in a lot of situations.

I made my screen from ash with ash veneer plywood panels. The finish is Watco Oil — an oil/varnish blend.

FOLDING SCREEN
inches (millimeters)

REFERENCE	QUANTITY	PART	STOCK	THICKNESS	(mm)	WIDTH	(mm)	LENGTH	(mm)
A	6	stiles/legs	hardwood	$7/8$	(22)	$2^1/4$	(57)	66	(1676)
B	6	rails	hardwood	$7/8$	(22)	$3^1/2$	(89)	$14^1/2$	(368)
C	3	panels	hardwood	$1/4$	(6)	$14^7/16$	(367)	$56^7/16$	(1434)

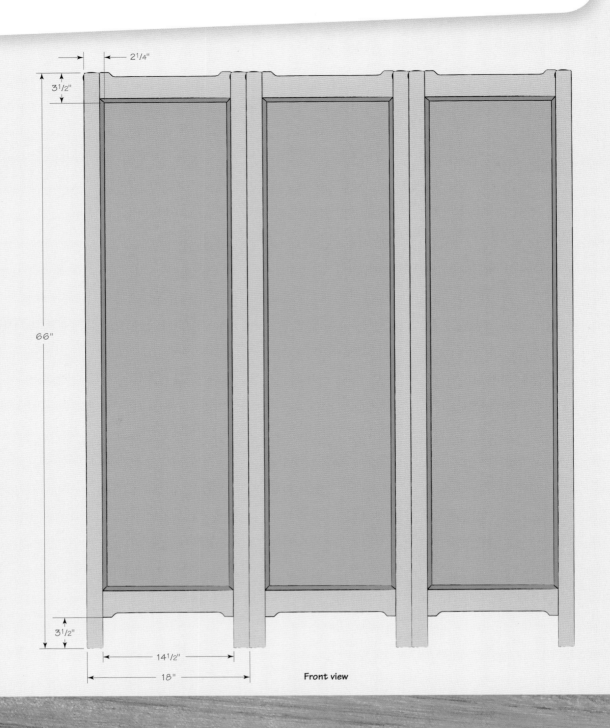

2$^1/4$"

3$^1/2$"

66"

3$^1/2$"

14$^1/2$"

18"

Front view

BIT BOX

EAGLE AMERICA CATALOG NO.

cope and stick, $\frac{1}{2}$" shank, No. 185-0900

pattern, $\frac{1}{2}$" shank, No. 102-1625B

1" straight, $\frac{1}{2}$" shank, No. 102-1625

HARDWARE

4   Folding screen hinges No. 8 w/screws
Lee Valley No. 00H53.03

Panel C (3)

Rail B (6)

Stile/leg A (6)

Hold-Down Fence

Most of the time, installing a set of hold downs on a router table is more trouble than it's worth. When you're working with cope-and-stick bits, or other bits where the profile created must match up very precisely with an adjacent part, they are part of an overall strategy to make those profiles as accurately as possible. I use a combination of commercial and shop-made featherboards when I have need for such a precise setup, although there is no reason you shouldn't make all of your own featherboards — the technique is certainly easy enough.

Start by cutting the featherboards to the size and shape indicated in the Featherboard Detail. Cut the grooves through the pieces on your router table. Draw a line across the piece at the same angle you cut on the end. The line should be about 4³/₄" from the end of the board. If you're using a standard, ¹/₈" kerf saw blade, set your saw to make a 2⁷/₈" cut and set the blade so it is about 1¹/₂" high. Cut in until the cut touches the line then carefully back the piece out of the cut. Bump the fence over ¹/₄" and make another cut to the line. Repeat the process, until you have cut fingers across the width of the featherboard piece.

It is critical that the feathers are each the same thickness, so the resistance they create is equal. This makes it easier to push workpieces past the boards in a fluid manner. If you are using a thin-kerf blade, the fence adjustment between each cut is twice the width of the kerf. You should also adjust the width of the featherboards to be an odd multiple of the kerf width. This will give you a feather at either edge of the board.

I typically make up feather boards from ash, oak or some other springy wood. Woods such as cherry and maple will work, but I make the feathers longer to compensate for their stiffness.

STEP 1 Cut the stiles and rails to sizes listed in the Materials List. Also, cut an extra piece or two the same thickness for testing the bit set up. Most cope-and-stick bit sets are designed to be used with ³/₄"-thick material. But, most will also accommodate stock that is a little thicker. I opted for using ⁷/₈" stock after the first pieces I cut warped badly when I milled them to ³/₄". The thicker material also seems a little more substantial in a freestanding piece such as this screen. Mark off ³/₁₆" on the end of one of the rails. Chuck the sticking bit (the one that makes the cut along the length of the pieces) in your table-mounted router. Adjust the bit's height so the corner of the square, grooving cutter hits your line.

STEP 2 Clamp an auxiliary hold-down fence to your standard router table fence. The hold-down fence is equipped with two shop-made feather boards that will help keep constant pressure on the pieces as you run them across the table. Plans for the fence are shown in Hold-Down Fence on the facing page.

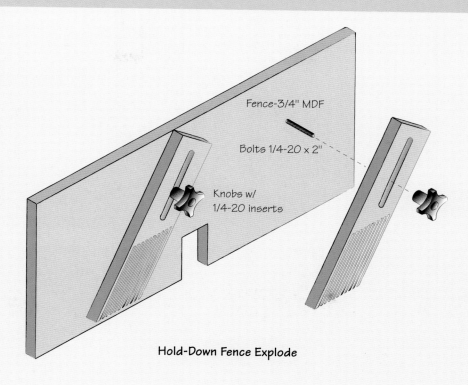

Fence-3/4" MDF

Bolts 1/4-20 x 2"

Knobs w/
1/4-20 inserts

Hold-Down Fence Explode

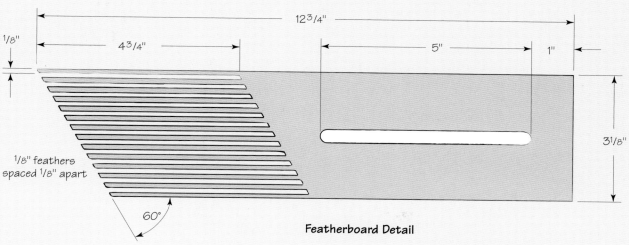

12³/4"

1/8"

4³/4"

5"

1"

1/8" feathers
spaced 1/8" apart

60°

3¹/8"

Featherboard Detail

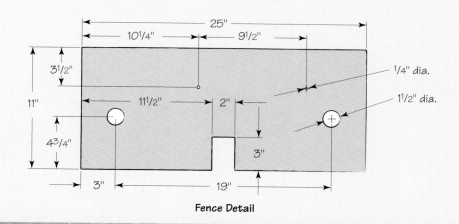

25"

10¹/4"

9¹/2"

3¹/2"

1/4" dia.

11"

11¹/2"

2"

1¹/2" dia.

4³/4"

3"

3"

19"

Fence Detail

STEP 3 Adjust the fence to makes its face tangent to the bit's bearing.

STEP 4 Hold one of the stiles along the fence and adjust the feather boards to put firm pressure down on it. The featherboards' feathers should be flexed slightly when you have the adjustment right. You also won't be able to back the piece out — it will only move forward. (Note: The featherboards I am using flat on the table are a commercial model that are designed to fit in a miter gauge slot — turning the knob not only locks the feather board at a specific angle, it also locks the unit in place in the slot. You could easily make featherboards of your own to clamp to the table.

STEP 5 Cut the pieces from right to left, trying to push each through the cut with as fluid a motion as possible. Watch carefully to make sure the pieces don't come up off the table, or move away from the fence. (Note: Cope-and-stick cutters are designed to cut the piece with their good side down on the table.)

STEP 6 Keep a push stick handy for feeding the last few inches of the stile past the bit. With the featherboards in place, you'll be pushing a little harder than usual. The push stick is cheap insurance should you happen to slip while applying the added pressure — at least your fingers won't come into contact with the whirling bit.

STEP 7 Make the sticking cut on one long edge of each rail. These pieces are enough smaller and easier to control that I didn't bother with the feather boards on the table. I also figured that as the cuts on the edges of the rails didn't have to mate with anything, they didn't need to be cut as precisely.

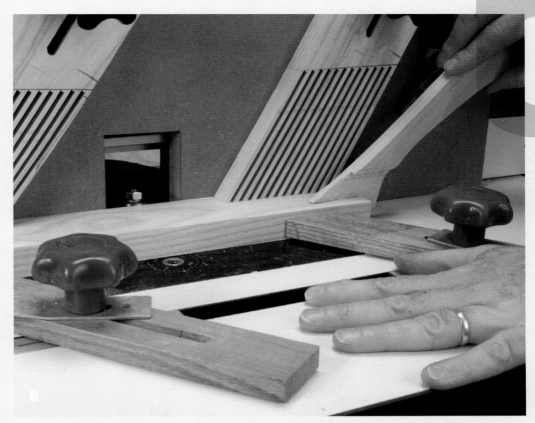

8

Coping Sleds

If you make a lot of frames using cope-and-stick bits, you may find it helpful to make or buy a coping sled. This is a carrier with a sliding table that rides in the miter gauge slot. Most have a fence that you can adjust to be square to the bit. A stop clamped to the fence controls the length of the pieces. The advantage to using a sled is that it eliminates having to guide the workpiece with its end running along the fence. Several companies, including Eagle America, sell such a sled, or you can make one as shown page 116.

I would have used that sled for the cuts on the screen rails, but I didn't make it until after the screen was finished.

STEP 8 Swap the sticking bit for the coping bit. Use one of the rail pieces to help adjust the bit's height. Adjust the bit so the lower corner of the square cutter aligns with the upper side of the groove.

STEP 9 Make a cut on one end of your test piece, using a push block to help guide the piece past the bit. Turn the piece over (so the shaped cut it up) and check the fit against one of the stiles. If the face of the test piece is proud of the face of the stile, lower the bit. If it is below the stile, raise the bit. Keep making test cuts until you are satisfied with the fit. Then, cut both ends of all six rails. Be careful not to let the pieces dip into the opening in the fence — they'll have a tendency to do that when the trailing edge leaves the fence on the infeed side of the fence.

9

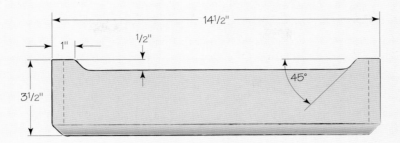

6

Screen Rail Detail

14 1/2"

1"

1/2"

45°

3 1/2"

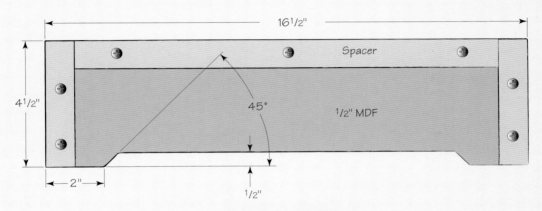

16 1/2"

4 1/2"

Spacer

45°

1/2" MDF

2"

1/2"

Screen-Template Detail

10

STEP 10 With the joinery cuts finished, it's time to start making the template for the step cuts on the rails. Cut the template piece to the size indicated in the Template Detail. Lay out the angled cuts as shown. Tip the blade on your table saw to 45° and make the cuts by standing the pieces on edge and guiding them with a miter gauge. A stop on the miter gauge's fence serves to position the cuts. Make the cut on one end of both pieces then turn the pieces around to make the second cuts.

STEP 11 To make the straight cut connecting the two angled cuts, adjust the fence so it is $1/2$" from the outside of the blade. Lower the blade beneath the table. Hold the template against the fence directly over the blade. Start the saw and slowly raise blade up through the template (be sure to hold onto the template as you bring the blade up). Push the template forward until the cut almost reaches the angled cut at the trailing end of the piece. Lower the blade and shut off the saw. Finish the cut with the band saw and clean up the template with a sharp chisel. Repeat these steps for the second template.

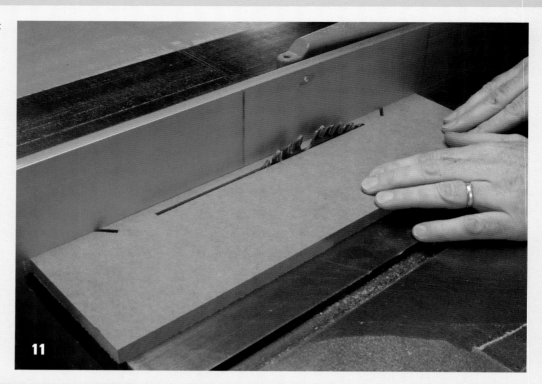

STEP 12 Drill both templates for screws as shown in the drawing. Center a rail on one of the templates and surround it with 1"-wide spacers that are the same thickness as the rail. Hold the spacers in place with double-faced tape. Add the second template to the top of the sandwich. Tape it in place as well. Then drill pilot holes and screw everything together. In addition to holding the pieces together while you are fastening them with screws, the tape also serves to create a little clearance inside the template so you can get the pieces in and out.

STEP 13 Drill a series of three holes through the back of the template. The center one is a $1/2$"-diameter hole that you can poke a dowel through in case one of the rails gets stuck inside. The other two holes are $3/16$"-diameter clearance holes for screws that will hold the rails in the jig while you rout. These need to be offset slightly to the back side of the template so the screws go into the grooves in the rails. Countersink the screw holes as a finishing touch and mark the template so you know which is the front side.

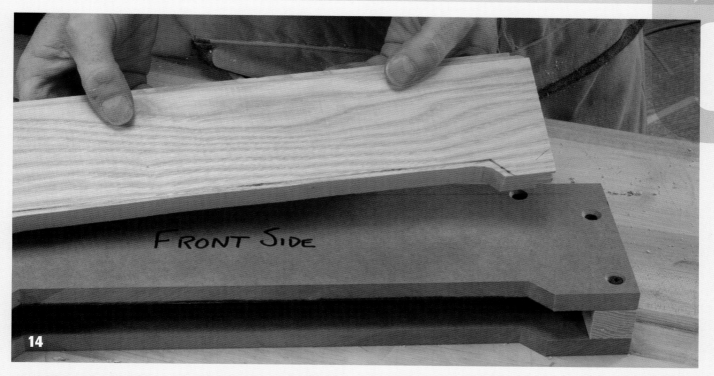

STEP 14 Slip each rail into the template and trace the cutout onto the rail's face. Cut away the bulk of the waste on the band saw, staying about $^1/_{16}$ -$^1/_8$" away from the line. This excess is especially important in the corners. The cut will be rounded rather than an actual angle as it is on the template.

STEP 15 Slide a rail into the template and secure it with screws. (Note: Be sure the front face of the rail is towards the labeled side of the template so the screws end up in the groove. Chuck a pattern bit in your table-mounted router and make the cut down the angled part of the template and along the straightaway. Stop about $^2/_3$ of the way across.

STEP 16 Flip the template over and cut the second side. The whole reason for making a two-sided template is that it allows you to make both of the angled cuts with the grain. If you tried to get away with a single-sided template, it is very likely that the rail would tear out badly as you cut the second angle.

STEP 17 Cut the molded edge off the bottom of each stile to form a foot. Start by making a shoulder cut on the table saw. The blade height should be set at $1/2$". Guide the pieces with the miter gauge. Use a piece of scrap against the rip fence to position the cut. Cut all six stiles, making sure to make three rights and three lefts.

STEP 18 After establishing the shoulder on the table saw, chuck a 1" straight bit in your table-mounted router and bury it behind the fence so only about $1/4$" is exposed. Position the stile to the left of the bit and pivot it into the cut, trying to cut as close to the saw cut as possible without going past it. Once the stile is against the fence, feed it to the left to cut away the molding.

STEP 19 After cutting all six stiles at the initial setting, adjust the fence to expose $1/2$" of the bit. Repeat the process, pivoting the pieces into the cut and then feeding them to the left. This should cut away all of the molding at the bottom of each stile except for a little bit right in the corner.

STEP 20 Make a clamping block from one of your test pieces. This will keep the clamp from damaging the molded edges of the stiles. Clamp the pieces to your bench and cut away the little bit of extra in the corner with a sharp chisel.

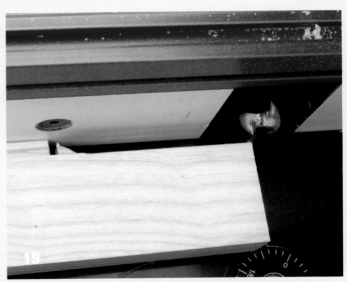

21

STEP 21 Cut the plywood panels to size. Glue up the individual frame sections. Be sure that the bottom rails are flush with the shoulder cut at the bottom of the stiles and that the top rails are flush with the top ends of the stiles. Be sure to insert the panels into their grooves. When the glue dries, sand the frames and apply finish.

STEP 22 Make a story stick about 9" long with a foot at one end. Hook the foot over the ends of the stiles and position the hinges at the other end. Hinge the three panels together.

22

coffee table

THE DESIGN for this coffee table grew out of a couple of details that I wanted to include in the book. The first is the wide bevel around the top. Credit for this (and the jig used to create it) must go to John Dodd, friend, teacher and fellow woodworker. John incorporated this bevel into the edge of a desk I helped him build one summer. On that piece, the bevel eased the edge of the writing surface, making it much friendlier for the user. The bevel looked really nice to boot and I stashed it away in my image bank waiting for an opportunity to use it. I also like it because it is a cut that is not obviously routed since it is so much wider than a typical router cut.

The other detail is the chamfered hole cut in each leg. I think this is the type of thing that elevates a design from being merely pleasing to being something quite special. It is fun to think that sometimes taking material away can be just as important as adding something on. While the hole itself is drilled, the chamfer is routed.

The rest of the table also makes good use of the router. The joinery is mortise and tenon (although there are half-laps where the stretchers meet in the center — cut on the table saw). And the two circle pieces are made with the help of a trammel jig. I used cherry for my table — it's hard to beat that warm red glow — although I did consider making the top from plywood with a plastic laminate surface. Had I gone that route, I would have made a segmented frame around the plywood and beveled that. A coffee table with a durable laminate surface has some obvious advantages, particularly if there are children in the house. Whatever way you go, choose a durable finish — regardless of who uses them, coffee tables take a lot of abuse.

COFFEE TABLE
inches (millimeters)

REFERENCE	QUANTITY	PART	STOCK	THICKNESS	(mm)	WIDTH	(mm)	LENGTH	(mm)
A	4	legs	hardwood	$1^{3/4}$	(45)	$3^{5/8}$	(92)	$15^{3/4}$	(400)
B	2	wide stretchers	hardwood	$1^{1/2}$	(38)	$2^{1/2}$	(64)	$31^{1/2}$	(800)
C	2	narrow stretchers	hardwood	$1^{1/2}$	(38)	$1^{1/2}$	(38)	$31^{1/2}$	(800)
D	1	tenon stock	hardwood	$1/2$	(13)	$1^{1/2}$	(38)	20	(508)
E	1	shelf	hardwood	$5/8$	(16)	$29^{1/2}$	(749)	$29^{1/2}$	(749)
F	1	top	hardwood	$1^{1/4}$	(32)	42	(1067)	42	(1067)

BIT BOX

EAGLE AMERICA CATALOG NO.

$1/2$" straight, $1/2$" shank, No. 102-0885

45° chamfer, $1/2$" shank, No. 152-0625

1" straight, $1/2$" shank, No. 102-1625

1" pattern, $1/2$" shank, No. 102-1625B

$1/8$" roundover, $1/4$" shank, No. 156-0202

$1/4$" roundover, $1/2$" shank, No. 156-0405

22.5° chamfer, $1/2$" shank, No. 152-0305

$1^{1/2}$" Forstner bit

HARDWARE

4   No.8 x 2" (50mm) flathead wood screws

4   No.8 x 3" (75mm) flathead wood screws

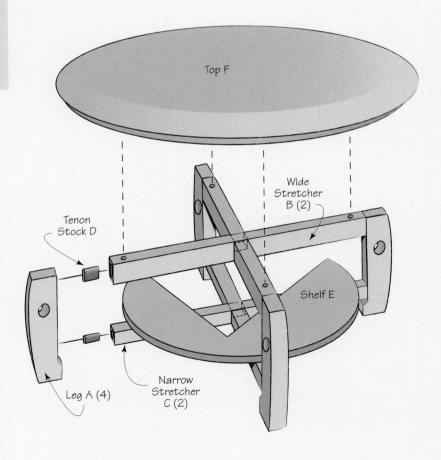

Top F

Tenon Stock D

Wide Stretcher B (2)

Shelf E

Leg A (4)

Narrow Stretcher C (2)

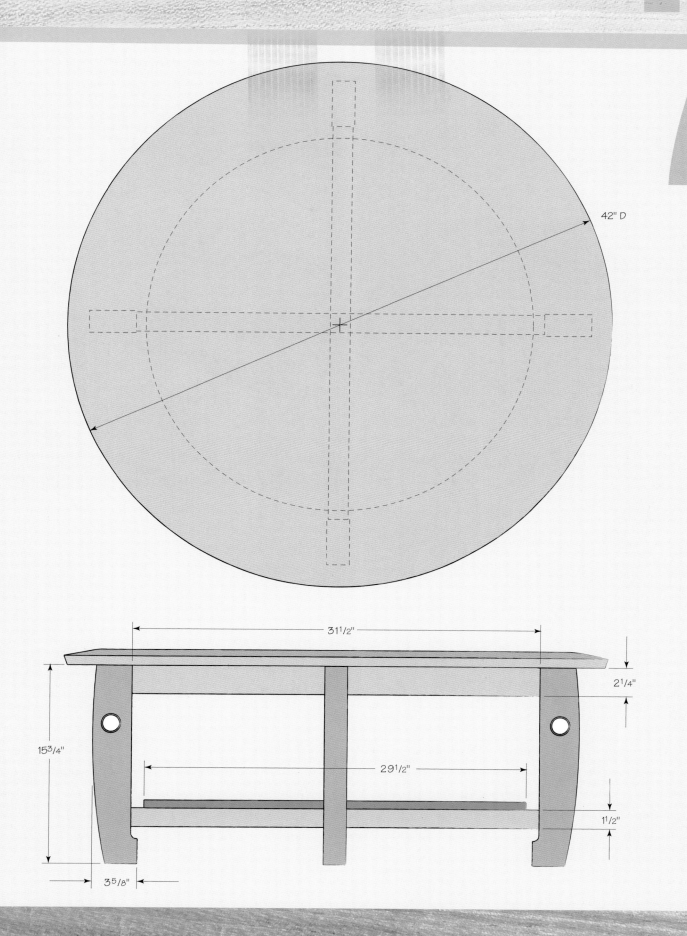

42" D

31¹/2"

2¹/4"

15³/4"

29¹/2"

1¹/2"

3⁵/8"

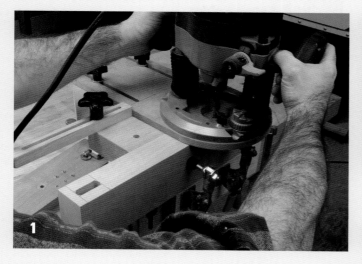

7

Leg Detail

STEP 1 Cut the legs to the size listed in the Materials List. Lay out the mortises on one leg as shown in the Leg Detail. Clamp the leg horizontally in the mortising jig. You will probably have to add a spacer to the horizontal fence to pack it out so the clamps will work on the thicker material. Chuck a 1/2" spiral upcut (or straight) bit in your plunge router. Use an edge guide to position the bit in the center the of the thickness of the leg. Set the stops on the jig to control the length of the mortises. Rout the mortises 1 1/2" deep. (I know it says 1" on the drawing — you'll be cutting away this excess material later.) Mortise all four legs.

STEP 2 Drill a 1 1/2"-diameter hole through each leg as shown in the Leg Detail. Back up the holes with a fresh piece of scrap to prevent the back side from tearing out.

STEP 3 Chuck a 45° chamfer bit in your table-mounted router. Set its height to make a chamfer that is about 3/16" wide. (Make a test cut first!) Start the router and place a table leg over the bit with the bearing sticking up into the hole. Run the leg around the bit to cut the chamfer. Chamfer both sides of the hole in each leg.

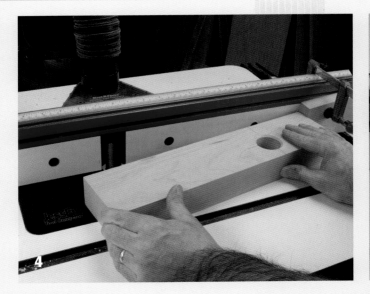

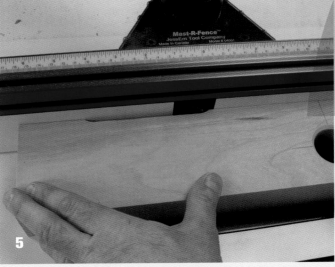

STEP 4 The foot at the bottom of each leg is created by routing away $1/2$" of material from the leg's back side. Start by chucking a long 1"-diameter pattern-cutting bit in your table-mounted router. Adjust the bit's height so it clears the top of the leg. Clamp a stop $13^1/4$" to the right of the bit as measured from the bit's center. Bury the bit behind the fence so it makes a cut about $1/8$" deep. Start the router and hold a leg with its upper end against the stop and the mortises pointed towards the fence. Pivot the leg into the cut until it is firmly against the fence.

STEP 5 Once the leg contacts the fence, push it from right to left to make the cut.

STEP 6 Stop routing when the cut reaches about $1/2$" from the end of the leg (or when the end of the leg threatens to drop into the opening surrounding the bit). Repeat the cut with the three other legs. Move the fence back, deepening the cut to $1/4$". Cut the legs again. Repeat the process, moving the fence $1/8$" at a time until the cut is $1/2$" deep.

STEP 7 I thought about all sorts of elaborate jigs that might serve to complete the cut on the back of each leg and finally decided the direct approach is best. Rather than trying to jig this operation for use with a router, cut the excess material away on the band saw and plane the surface flush with a block plane.

Drawing Curves

Laying out a true or *fair* curve can be tough. One trick I use a lot is to make a drawing spline from a thin (¹/₈") strip of straight-grained wood. (The more uniform the grain pattern is, the more evenly the piece will bend.) Drill a hole at either end and run a string between them. Tightening the string produces a uniform bend in the strip that you can trace to make your layout.

STEP 8 Lay out the curve on one of the legs as shown in the Leg Detail. The exact shape isn't critical — just try to hit the points at the top and bottom of the leg that are dimensioned on the drawing. Cut a piece of MDF or plywood to use as a pattern. I used a thicker piece (1") because I had it, although the added thickness is nice because you will be driving screws into its edges. Hold the leg on the pattern with its top flush with one end of the pattern and its back flush with one side. Trace the rectangular shape of the leg onto the pattern, then lay out the curve as you did on the leg. I like to do both layouts because it helps me visualize the shape I'm after. Cut the pattern out on the band saw and sand it to final shape.

STEP 9 Orient the pattern so the bottom end of the leg points to the right. Screw fences to the top end and the back side of the pattern. Hold the leg in the resulting cradle and trace the curve onto its side. Rough-cut the curve on the band saw to remove most of the waste. Clamp the leg to the pattern. (Use a little scrap as a pad inside the hole to avoid scarring the leg with the clamp.) Chuck your pattern-cutting bit in your table-mounted router and adjust it so it cuts the full thickness of the leg. Start the router and pivot the jig up against the bit at about the leg's midpoint. Rout the lower part of the leg moving the pattern/leg from right to left.

STEP 10 Rout the lower part of the other three legs. Then reattach the fences so they cradle the piece on the opposite side of the pattern. Rout the upper part of each leg with this new jig configuration. All this bother is about orienting the leg so the bit is cutting with the grain. If you tried to cut the whole curve in one pass, the cut on one side of the curve or the other would be against the grain and might tear out.

STEP 11 Reconfigure your mortising jig with the vertical fence. Again, you'll need to add a spacer so the clamps will work with the thicker stock. Notice how I cut dadoes in my spacer so it would fit over the bolts that hold the fence to the front of the jig. Center the mortises on the stock with the help of the edge guide, and use the stops on the jig to control the length of the mortises. Mortise both ends of both stretchers.

STEP 12 Both pairs of stretchers meet in a half-lap joint where they intersect at the center of the table. While you could cut these notches with a router, a dado blade on the table saw is far more efficient. Lay out the joints and adjust the height of the dado so it cuts halfway through the pieces. Guide the pieces past the blade with a miter gauge. Use a stop on the gauge to help position the cuts. Cut half the notch, then turn the piece around to make the other half of the cut. Start by making the notch too small and gradually increase its width.

13

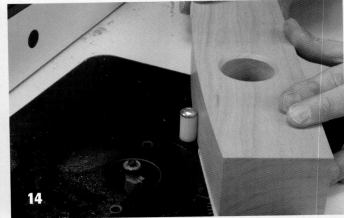

14

STEP 13 Chuck a 1/8" roundover bit in your table-mounted router and position the fence tangent with the bit's bearing. Round over all four edges on the narrow stretches and the bottom two edges on the wide stretchers.

STEP 14 While you have the roundover bit in position, also round over all four edges on each leg. Because the legs are curved, you'll have to guide them against the bit's bearing, rather than using the fence. Attach a starting pin (the bolt with the white collar) to your router table. Start the router and pivot the leg on the starting pin until it comes in contact with the bearing. Then push the leg through the cut — you don't have to keep the piece in contact with the starting pin once you have made contact with the bearing.

STEP 15 Cut lengths of tenon stock to fit in the mortises. Switch to a 1/4" roundover bit and round over the corners. Cut the tenon stock into individual tenons, each 2" long.

15

Small Adjustments

When you need to remove just a tiny bit more material, it is often easier to insert a shim beside the stop, rather than trying to move the stop itself. Plastic-coated playing cards work well for this as they are of very uniform thickness (.01").

16

STEP 16 Glue up narrower boards to make a panel wide enough for the shelf. Locate the center on the underside and drill a 1/4" hole, 1/2" deep. Attach the Large Router Trammel to your plunge router, and chuck up a 1/2" spiral upcut bit. Put the trammel's pivot pin in the hole and adjust the trammel to make a 29⁵/8"-diameter circle. Make the cut in several shallow passes. Once you cut the circle completely, reset the trammel to 29¹/2" and make a final, trim pass.

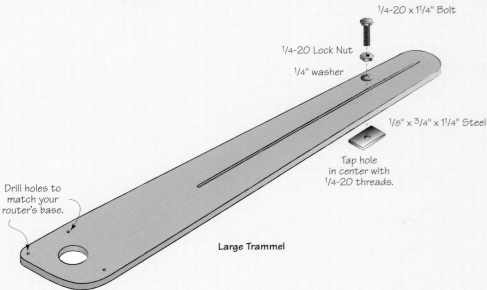

1/4-20 x 1¹/4" Bolt

1/4-20 Lock Nut

1/4" washer

1/8" x 3/4" x 1¹/4" Steel

Tap hole in center with 1/4-20 threads.

Drill holes to match your router's base.

Large Trammel

Large Router Trammel

You don't have to do a lot of curved work before you realize that circles (or parts thereof) are easier to layout than curves that don't come from a circle. The reason is based in geometry – a circle has a fixed center point. Because of this fact, you can easily lay out and cut most curves if you have a big enough compass. (For a while, I had a compass rigged up in my shop that would cut a 12 foot radius – it worked, though not without a lot of gymnastics on my part.) The trammel (a fancy name for a compass) shown here will cut circles from 24 inches up to about 60 inches in diameter. It makes a nice companion to the small trammel shown on page 67. As with most of my jigs, I made this from a piece of scrap left over from another project, so the scrap's size dictated the jig's size. Feel free to alter the dimensions to fit your scraps, your current project or your whim. Follow the plans and you'll soon have a router trammel that can cut fine circles.

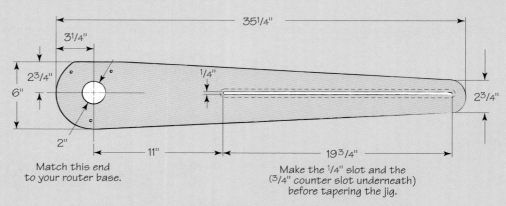

Match this end to your router base.

Make the 1/4" slot and the (3/4" counter slot underneath) before tapering the jig.

**Large Trammel
Top View**

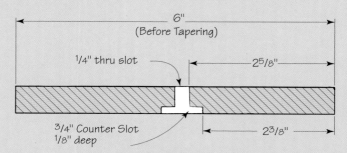

6"
(Before Tapering)

1/4" thru slot

2⁵/₈"

3/4" Counter Slot
1/8" deep

2³/₈"

**Large Trammel
Cross Section**

17

18

STEP 17 Chuck the 1/8" roundo-ver bit in a handheld router and round over both of the shelf's edges. This is a great place to use one of the smaller, trim routers.

STEP 18 Glue the stretcher pairs together, checking to make sure they are square to one an-other. Drill screw holes through the stretchers as shown in the Stretcher Cross Section. Be sure to counterbore one of the stretchers from the topside as shown to allow the shelf to ex-pand and contract with changes in the weather. Center the nar-row stretchers on the underside of the shelf. Screw the stretch-ers in place, making sure the stretcher with the counterbores runs across the grain.

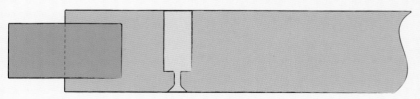

1/2" Dia. Counterbore
to allow for wood movement

3/8" Dia. Countersink
3/16" Dia. Clearance Hole

Stretcher Cross Section

STEP 19 Cut some angled clamp blocks as shown and screw them to a length of thin, flexible material such as Masonite. Be sure the screw heads are well recessed in the Masonite so they don't mar the legs. Apply glue to the mortises and tenons. Fit the pieces together and clamp. I found it easier to glue two opposing legs at a time rather than trying for all four because there wasn't enough room for the clamps to cross in the center. I did, however, fit the non-glued legs in place to keep things in alignment. I also found it easier to work with the table upside down. I added a partial sheet of MDF to my bench for added support.

STEP 20 Glue up stock for the top. Cut the top in a circle with the trammel as you did with the shelf. Chuck a 22.5° chamfer bit in a hand-held router and rout a chamfer around the underside of the disk. The chamfer should be about $3/4$" wide.

STEP 21 Make up a router carrier as shown in Bevel Jig on page 104. Chuck a long, 1"-diameter straight bit in the router and attach the router to the jig. (You need a long bit to account for the thickness of the jig.) Adjust the slide on the jig so the bit cuts along the edge of the coffee table top as shown in the Bevel Detail. Make the first cut about $1/4$" deep. Hold the jig flat on the table top and guide it with the dowels riding along the top's edge. Make a second pass to cut to the full depth — about $1/2$". Leave a slight flat ($1/8$" +/-) between the bevel and the intial, 22.5° chamfer. Save this $1/2$" depth setting.

STEP 22 Adjust the slide to position the bit for the second cut. Again, you may need to make this cut in two passes. Be sure to make the final pass at the same depth you used for the first cut. (Moving the sliding table automatically makes the second cut shallower.)

STEP 23 Loosen the wing nuts and move the slide to position the bit for the final pass. Start the router and plunge it down to its final depth — this cut is shallow enough to make in a single pass. Rout around the table top to finish the bevel. (Note: Be sure to hold the jig securely on the table top — with the bevel cut, the jig won't have a lot of support, especially near the edge.)

22

23

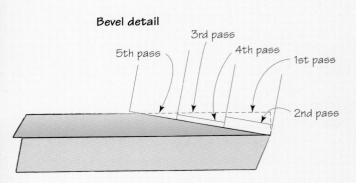

Bevel detail

5th pass 3rd pass 4th pass 1st pass

2nd pass

Bevel Jig

The wide bevel on the tabletop is made by running a router around the top when it is tilted. The jig holds the router at the proper tilt, and adjusts to make it easy to keep the bit at the proper depth. As with most jigs, the dimensions of the pieces aren't critical — use what you have on hand. Even the angle of the wedge is negotiable — if you make it steeper, the bevel gets narrower, if you make it shallower, the bevel will be wider. I mounted my router by setting it on the jig and running screws down through some existing holes in the router's base. If your router doesn't have these holes, unscrew the plastic base and use it as a pattern to drill mounting holes from the underside of the slide.

One of the neat features of this jig is that it will work on any diameter circle (down to about 12 inches in diameter). It will also work on straight edges, and might work with concave edges as well (I suspect it will, though I've never tried). The two-pin guidance system is a good one to keep in mind for other kinds of router sleds.

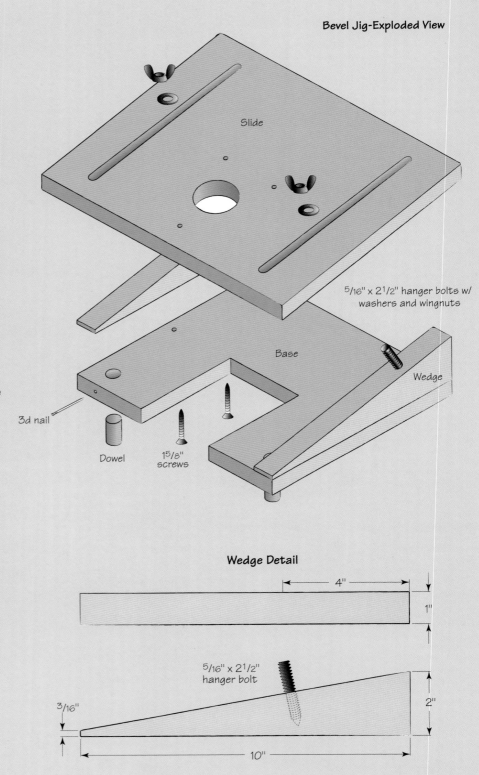

Bevel Jig-Exploded View

Slide

5/16" x 2¹/2" hanger bolts w/ washers and wingnuts

Base

Wedge

3d nail

Dowel

1⁵/8" screws

Wedge Detail

4"

1"

5/16" x 2¹/2" hanger bolt

3/16"

2"

10"

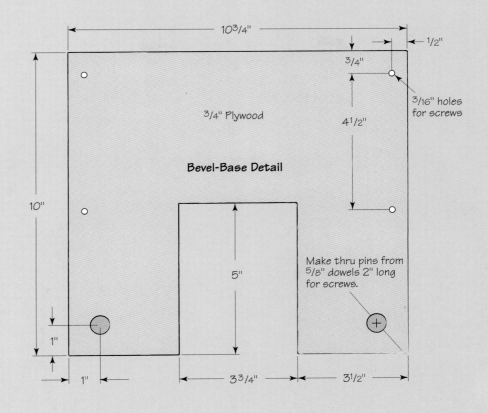

10³/₄"

1/2"

3/4"

3/16" holes
for screws

4¹/₂"

3/4" Plywood

Bevel-Base Detail

10"

5"

Make thru pins from
5/8" dowels 2" long
for screws.

1"

1"

3³/₄"

3¹/₂"

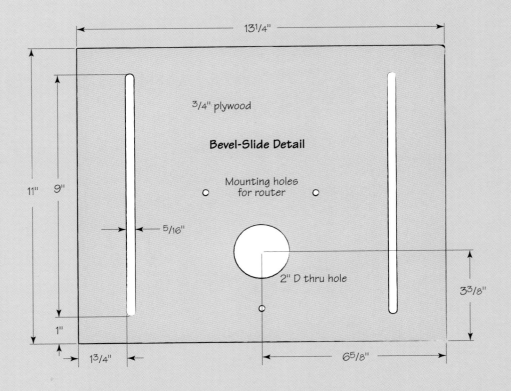

13¹/₄"

3/4" plywood

Bevel-Slide Detail

11"

9"

Mounting holes
for router

5/16"

2" D thru hole

3³/₈"

1"

1³/₄"

6⁵/₈"

collector's cabinet

YOU JUST NEVER KNOW when inspiration will strike. I was in a duty-free shop along the US-Canada border when I stumbled across a display stand similar to the cabinet shown in the photograph. The cabinet in the shop was being used to sell Canadian memorabilia and other souvenir trinkets. It wasn't especially well made, and it was painted black. But I remember thinking that if you spent a little extra time building the piece, and made it out of an attractive wood, it would make a stunning way to display a collection.

I borrowed my wife's cell phone (now I realize why a phone with a camera is a useful thing) and shot a couple quick photos so I would have something to jog my memory when I returned home. After playing around with the proportions, I arrived at the design presented here. The dark wood is jatoba, a South American hardwood sometimes billed as Brazilian cherry. The drawer fronts are curly maple, and the rest of the drawers, regular maple. Tempered glass shelves complete the unit up above.

As for construction, this piece uses almost the full array of router joinery. The drawer case is assembled with lock miters and dadoes. The hoops require miters and mortise and tenon joints, while the drawers are dovetailed.

COLLECTOR'S CABINET
inches (millimeters)

REFERENCE	QUANTITY	PART	STOCK	THICKNESS	(mm)	WIDTH	(mm)	LENGTH	(mm)
A	1	top	hardwood	5/8	(16)	15	(381)	54	(1372)
B	2	sides	hardwood	5/8	(16)	15	(381)	7 1/2	(191)
C	1	bottom	hardwood	5/8	(16)	15	(381)	53	(1346)
D	2	dividers	hardwood	5/8	(16)	15	(381)	5	(127)
E	3	back panels	hardwood	1/2	(13)	5	(127)	17 7/16	(443)
F	24	plugs	hardwood			3/8D	(10)	1/2	(13)
G	16	segments	hardwood	7/8	(22)	4	(102)	19 3/4	(502)
H	2	tenon stock	hardwood	3/8	(10)	1 3/4	(45)	16	(406)
J	4	upper spreaders	hardwood	3/4	(19)	2 1/4	(57)	11 5/8	(295)
K	2	lower spreaders	hardwood	3/4	(19)	2 1/2	(64)	11 5/8	(295)
L	2	tenon stock	hardwood	3/8	(10)	1 1/2	(38)	16	(406)
M	3	drawer fronts	hardwood	3/4	(19)	4 3/4	(121)	17 3/16	(437)
N	6	drawer sides	hardwood	1/2	(13)	4 3/4	(121)	14	(356)
P	3	drawer backs	hardwood	1 1/4	(32)	4	(102)	17 3/16	(437)
Q	3	drawer bottoms	hardwood	1/4	(6)	13 11/16	(348)	16 11/16	(424)
R	3	drawer stops	hardwood	1/4	(6)	3/4	(19)	3	(76)

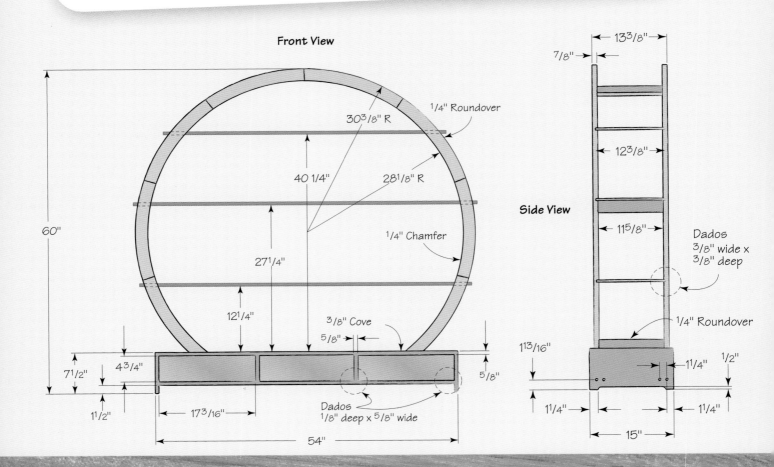

Front View

1/4" Roundover
30 3/8" R
28 1/8" R
1/4" Chamfer
40 1/4"
27 1/4"
60"
12 1/4"
3/8" Cove
5/8"
7 1/2"
4 3/4"
1 1/2"
17 3/16"
5/8"
Dados 1/8" deep x 5/8" wide
54"

Side View

13 3/8"
7/8"
12 3/8"
11 5/8"
Dados 3/8" wide x 3/8" deep
1/4" Roundover
1 13/16"
1 1/4"
1/2"
1 1/4"
1 1/4"
1 1/4"
15"

BIT BOX

EAGLE AMERICA CATALOG NO.

lock miter, $\frac{1}{2}$" shank, No. 192-2815

$\frac{5}{8}$" straight, $\frac{1}{2}$" shank, No. 102-1035

$\frac{3}{8}$" straight, $\frac{1}{2}$" shank, No. 102-0645

1" straight, $\frac{1}{2}$" shank, No. 102-1225

$\frac{3}{8}$" spiral upcut, $\frac{1}{2}$" shank, No. 106-0615

$\frac{3}{16}$" roundover, $\frac{1}{4}$" shank, No. 156-0302

$\frac{1}{2}$" spiral upcut, $\frac{1}{2}$" shank, No. 106-0835

flush trim, $\frac{1}{4}$" shank, No. 117-0822

$\frac{1}{4}$" roundover, $\frac{1}{2}$" shank, No. 156-0405

45° chamfer, $\frac{1}{2}$" shank, No. 152-0655

dovetail, to suit jig

$\frac{1}{4}$" straight, $\frac{1}{4}$" shank, No. 102-0442

$\frac{3}{8}$" cove, $\frac{1}{4}$" shank, No. 154-0602

$\frac{3}{8}$" plug cutter

HARDWARE

24 No. 8 x 2$\frac{1}{2}$" (65mm) flathead wood screws

4 No. 8 x 1$\frac{1}{4}$" (30mm) brass roundhead wood screws

3 drawer pulls, Lee Valley No.01W37.60

3 $\frac{3}{8}$" (10mm) x 12$\frac{7}{16}$" (316mm) x 48$\frac{7}{8}$" (1241mm) tempered glass shelves

57$\frac{1}{2}$" (1461mm)

60" (1524mm)

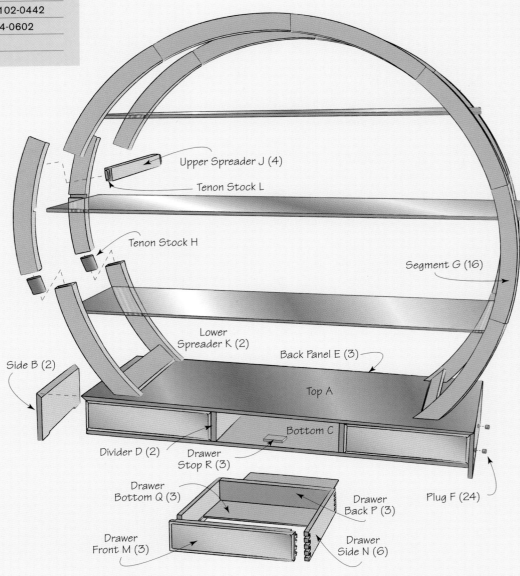

Upper Spreader J (4)

Tenon Stock L

Tenon Stock H

Segment G (16)

Lower Spreader K (2)

Back Panel E (3)

Side B (2)

Top A

Bottom C

Divider D (2)

Drawer Stop R (3)

Plug F (24)

Drawer Bottom Q (3)

Drawer Back P (3)

Drawer Front M (3)

Drawer Side N (6)

COLLECTOR'S CABINET

MAKING THE DRAWER UNIT

STEP 1 Cut the top, bottom, sides and dividers to the sizes listed in the Materials List. You may need to edge glue narrower boards to make up the wider width pieces. The top corners of the drawer unit are joined with a lock miter joint. Getting this bit set up correctly requires a series of successive approximations. Chuck a lock-miter bit in your table-mounted router. Mark the center of one of the pieces and adjust the bit height as shown. You're trying to align the center line with a point midway down the slightly sloped part of the bit. This should get you close to the right setting.

STEP 2 To test the bit height, you'll need to position the fence in about the right place. I used a shop-made fence for these cuts as I can screw my Board Buddies (hold-downs) right to its top surface. Hold a test piece vertically against the fence and adjust the fence until it appears as though the cut will leave a very slight flat where the test piece meets the table. Clamp the fence in place.

STEP 3 Hold the test piece flat on the table and make a test cut. Rip a slice off the edge of the board, flip it over and fit the joint together. Ideally, the surfaces will be flush. If they're not, you'll need to adjust the bit height. If the pointy part of the joint falls below the surface of the mating piece (as shown) you'll need to lower the bit. If the pointy part of the joint is above the mating surface, raise the bit. In either case, the adjustment needed will be half of the error the test pieces indicate.

STEP 4 Once the bit height is set, you can fine tune the fence position. Ideally, you want the cut to leave a knife edge on the workpiece without cutting away too much material (which will alter the dimensions of the stock. Cut another test piece partway and check. If the bit leaves a slight flat, move the fence away from you, exposing more of the bit. If you seem to be cutting too much material, move the fence toward you. Once the fence is set, cut the sides with the pieces held vertically against the fence.

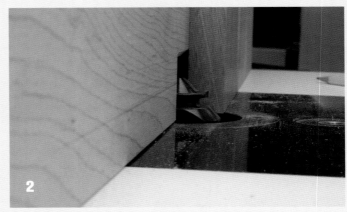

STEP 5 Cut the miters on the top with the piece held flat on the router table. This is an awkward cut as the top is quite large. I invested in a set of Board Buddies, spring-loaded feed rollers that help hold things down on the table. You could also use featherboards. A roller stand or a helper on the other end of the piece will also make life easier.

STEP 6 Set up a 5/8" straight bit in your table-mounted router and cut dadoes across the sides for the bottom. The depth of cut should be about 1/8". Position the dadoes as shown in the Front View.

STEP 7 Clamp the sides to the top so you can get an accurate measurement for the length of the bottom. Cut the bottom to length. Lay out the locations of the dados for the dividers on both the underside of the top and the top side of the bottom. Clamp a straightedge along the layout line to prepare to rout the divider dadoes. For more about how to make a straightedge, see Enhanced Straightedges on page 59.

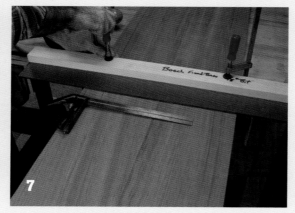

Precision Fence Adjustments

Matching material thickness to the diameter of a router bit can be a finicky operation. Rather than spend time going for an exact match, I often opt to leave the material a little on the thick side, then move my fences to compensate. To move a fence a precise amount, butt stops up against the fence on the side opposite of the direction you want to move the fence. Clamp the stops in place. Unclamp the fence and insert playing cards between it and the stops. For each card you use, you'll move the fence .01". Reclamp the fence to lock it in place.

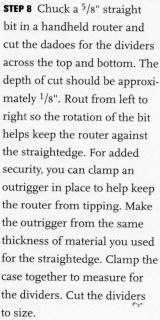

STEP 8 Chuck a ⁵/₈" straight bit in a handheld router and cut the dadoes for the dividers across the top and bottom. The depth of cut should be approximately ¹/₈". Rout from left to right so the rotation of the bit helps keep the router against the straightedge. For added security, you can clamp an outrigger in place to help keep the router from tipping. Make the outrigger from the same thickness of material you used for the straightedge. Clamp the case together to measure for the dividers. Cut the dividers to size.

STEP 9 Chuck a ³/₈" straight bit in your table-mounted router and set the depth of cut to ¹/₈". Position the fence ¹/₄" from the fence and cut grooves in the dividers for the back panels. Again, I used a shop-made fence for this operation so I could use my Board Buddies for the next step without having to change the setup.

STEP 10 Rout grooves in the top, bottom and sides with the same setup. When cutting the top and bottom, using hold downs or feather boards will help you control the pieces. (Note: When you cut grooves in the sides, you should stop when they intersect the dados you cut for the bottom.)

STEP 11 Cut the back panels to size. Chuck a ⁵/₈" straight bit in your table-mounted router and rabbet the back panels to fit in their grooves. The position of the fence controls the width of the rabbet, while the depth of the cut controls the thickness of the resulting tongue.

Only a Single Stop?

When I first set up to cut the feet on the sides, I tried using two stops — one at either end of the fence. This was a big mistake. With the workpiece against a stop at its trailing end, I carefully pivoted it into the cut only to have the bit grab the piece and tear out a chunk of material. I quickly shut down the router and took a minute to regroup. I figured out that because the cut was starting against the grain, and the wood (jatoba) was so dense, it was not going to cut well if I started this way.

So I decided to use just a single stop and make the foot cuts in two stages, flipping the piece over in between. This proved much more satisfactory. As a bonus, using a single stop made it a snap to make the cut symmetrical.

12A

STEP 12A The sides have a shallow cut on their bottom ends. These cuts create feet at the four corners of the unit which help it sit flatter on the floor. Start by chucking a 1" straight bit in your table-mounted router. Set the depth of cut so the bit cuts across the full thickness of the sides. Bury the bit in the fence, leaving about $1/8$" exposed. Clamp a stop $12^1/2$" away from the left-hand side of the bit. Start the cut by holding the leading end of the side against the fence midway between the bit and the stop.

STEP 12B Pivot the side until the trailing end makes contact with the fence. Feed the side along the fence until it contacts the stop.

STEP 12C When the piece contacts the stop, carefully pivot it away from the bit. Flip the side over to make the second part of the cut. To increase the depth of the foot, move the fence back, exposing more of the bit.

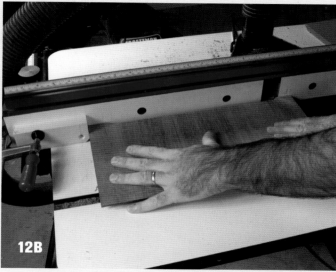

12B

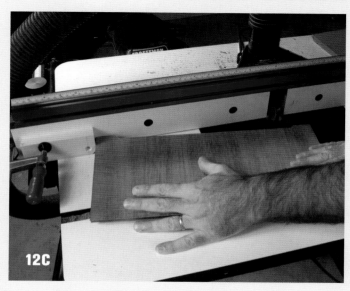

12C

STEP 13 Drill holes in the sides, top, and bottom for the screws that help hold the pieces together, Drill 3/8" counterbores first, then 3/16" clearance holes through the pieces for the screws.

STEP 14 Glue, clamp and screw the case together. Don't forget to put the back panels in place before putting everything together. You may want to prefinish the back panels before glue up. This makes finishing the case easier down the road.

MAKING THE HOOPS

STEP 1 The hoops each consist of six individual segments, mitered at the appropriate angles and joined with mortise and loose tenon joints. Rough-cut the miter on one end of each segment. Chuck a 1" straight bit in your table-mounted router and adjust the bit's height so it cuts across the full thickness of the segments. Set the miter jig for a 72 1/4° angle and trim the cut ends precisely. Use a stop to help ensure consistency.

Setting an Angle

When it comes to setting up for precise angles, it is hard to beat a tool called the Bevel Boss. This finely-made measuring device has markings that divide angles into 1/4° increments. It's available from many of the mail-order tool suppliers.

STEP 2 Rough-cut the second end of the pieces and trim them length with the same router set up. This time, use an adjustable stop so you can sneak up on the precise length required. Plans for both the Miter Jig and the Adjustable Stop are on pages 116-117.

Routed Miter Joints?

Why cut miters with a router? I find that despite investing in a high-quality blade for my miter saw, it still doesn't make a smooth enough cut for good joinery in dense hardwoods such as jatoba. You might try your table saw, but unless you have a really precise miter gauge, getting consistent, accurate result can be troublesome. Besides, this is a router book…

Note: This miter jig works well on the table saw too.

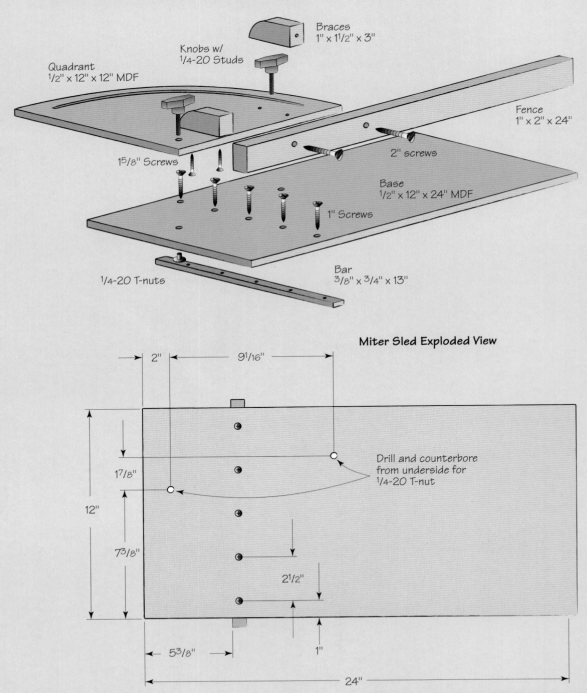

Braces
1" x 1¹/2" x 3"

Knobs w/
¹/4-20 Studs

Quadrant
¹/2" x 12" x 12" MDF

Fence
1" x 2" x 24"

1⁵/8" Screws

2" screws

Base
¹/2" x 12" x 24" MDF

1" Screws

¹/4-20 T-nuts

Bar
³/8" x ³/4" x 13"

Miter Sled Exploded View

2"

9¹/16"

Drill and counterbore
from underside for
¹/4-20 T-nut

1⁷/8"

12"

7³/8"

2¹/2"

5³/8"

1"

24"

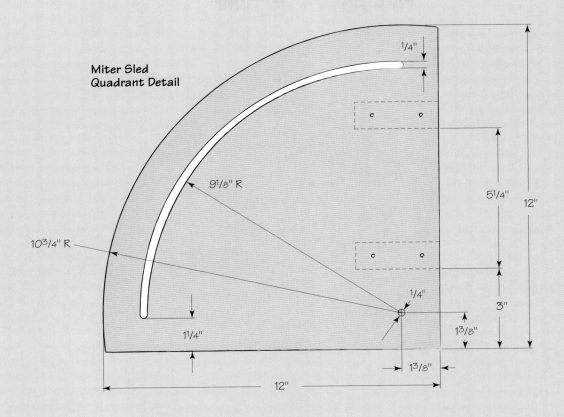

Miter Sled Quadrant Detail

1/4"

9 1/8" R

10 3/4" R

5 1/4"

12"

3"

1/4"

1 3/8"

1 3/8"

1 1/4"

12"

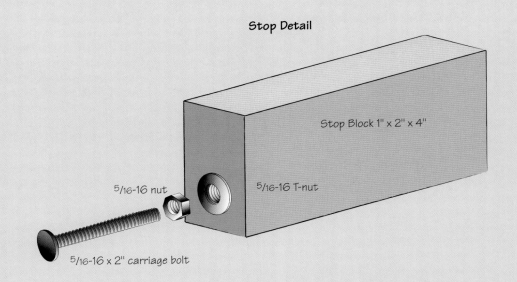

Stop Detail

Stop Block 1" x 2" x 4"

5/16-16 T-nut

5/16-16 nut

5/16-16 x 2" carriage bolt

STEP 3 Make an angled fence to bolt to the front of the Mortising Jig. (Plans for the jig are on page 36). Mark one face of all the segments. Mortise one end of each segment with a $^3/_8$" spiral upcut bit. Clamp the segments in place with the marked side against the jig.

STEP 4 Flip the fence over (you'll have to switch the clamps from side to side as well) to set up to mortise the opposite ends of the segments. Again, load each piece with the marked side against the jig. Staying consistent with the way the pieces are loaded into the jig means that even if the mortises are off center, they will all be off in the same direction and will still go together properly.

STEP 5 Cut 16"-long lengths of tenon stock to the proper width and thickness. Shape the corners with a $^3/_{16}$" roundover bit. Crosscut the tenons to the proper length. To determine this length, add together the depths of the mating mortises and subtract $^1/_{16}$" for insurance.

STEP 6 Cut a $2^1/_2$"-wide by 7"-long clamp block for each segment. Cut angles on the ends to match the angled cuts on the ends of the segments. Center the blocks along the outside edge of each segment and glue them in place. (Don't worry about the glue; you'll be cutting away this surface later.)

STEP 7 Swab glue in the mortises and on the tenons and glue up pairs of segments. I put a partial sheet of MDF down on my workbench to provide a large flat surface upon which to work. This large expanse will come in handy as the hoops come together.

STEP 8 If you have enough clamps, you can glue up the entire hoop at once. If not, glue up the pairs, then glue the pairs to the pairs together and so on. You can see where the large MDF surface comes in handy.

STEP 9 Here's where the MDF surface become a crucial part of the process. In order to cut the hoop to its final shape, you'll need to create a fixed center point to use with the router trammel (compass). Start by locating a center point 22" in from one edge of the sheet. This edge now becomes your reference edge. Drill a 1/4" hole in the center of a center block (a piece of cutoff from one of the segments works well because it's the right thickness) and screw it in place over the center point.

Fine Tuning Tenons

Sometimes loose tenons don't fit exactly as they should. I prefer to cut them a little on the snug side, because I can always make them a little smaller — if they start out too small, it's hard to make them bigger. To fine tune their fit, rub them on a sheet of sandpaper.

10

11

STEP 10 Clamp the hoop to the MDF surface with the inside corners of its opening aligned with the reference edge. Also center the hoop from side to side in relationship to the center block. Once you have the hoop positioned, you can screw it in place through the clamp blocks. Attach a big trammel (plans are on page 100) to your router and adjust it to make a 28$^1/8$"-diameter cut (as measured to the outside edge of the router bit). I used a $^1/2$" spiral upcut bit to make the cut, but any robust straight bit will work. Cut the inside of the hoop round in several light passes, pivoting the router in a clockwise direction. Leave about $^1/16$" of material at the bottom of the cut to avoid routing into the MDF.

STEP 11 Reset the trammel to make a 30$^3/8$"-diameter cut as measured to the inside edge of the bit. Rout the outside of the hoop in several light passes, rotating the router in a counter-clockwise direction. Again, leave about $^1/16$" of material at the bottom of the cut.

STEP 12 Rough cut the ends of the hoop close to the reference edge of the MDF with a jig saw. Make the final cut on each end with a flush trim bit. (Note: When I mortised the segments, I mortised both ends of all the pieces so I wouldn't have to keep track of which ones were the end pieces.

STEP 13 Unscrew the hoop from the MDF and turn it over. Rout away the excess material you left on both the inside and the outside of the hoop with a flush trim bit. I used a jig saw to cut away a lot of the excess material (including the clamp blocks) on the outside before routing.

12

13

STEP 14 The hoops are fastened together with a series of spreaders. These are joined to the hoops with mortise and loose tenon joints. Lay out the locations of the spreaders and the mortises around both hoops as shown in the Hoop Details. To make sure the locations match on both hoops, start with the hoops one on top of the other with both outside faces down. Lay out where the sides of the spreaders will fall, along with a center line for each. Use a square to transfer the marks down both the outside and inside edges. (Note: If you've ever wondered what the funny, angled head that came with your combination square was for, now's your chance to use it. It's called a center-finder and will allow you to draw radial lines across the surface of the hoop. Make the layouts for half the spreaders, then flip the top hoop over so the two inside faces are now together. Use the marks on the inside and outside edges to lay out the rest of the spreader locations on both hoops.

STEP 15 To rout the mortise for the spreaders, you'll need a straightedge to serve as a guide for the router. What's more, this straightedge has to be parallel to a line drawn tangent to the curve of the hoop. This isn't as difficult to achieve as it sounds. Make a V-shaped block as shown in the photo and in the Hoop Jig Detail. Lay out the V and cut it carefully on the band saw. This will serve in much the same way the center finder worked for making the layout. Drill holes through the MDF so you can clamp the hoops in place.

STEP 16 To align the hoop with the straightedge, hold the hoop so it touches both ends of the V. Slide it from side to side until the center line you drew earlier aligns with a line drawn through the center of the V. Clamp the hoop down to hold it in position. (Note: The curved block is there to help support the router as you work — it should be positioned about $1/2$" away from the inside edge of the hoop to keep it from interfering with the alignment.

14

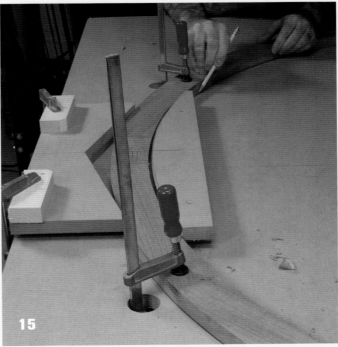

15

16

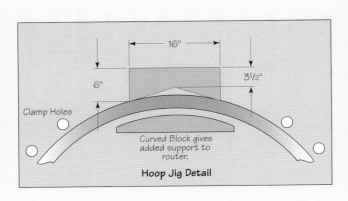

16"

6"

3 1/2"

Clamp Holes

Curved Block gives added support to router.

Hoop Jig Detail

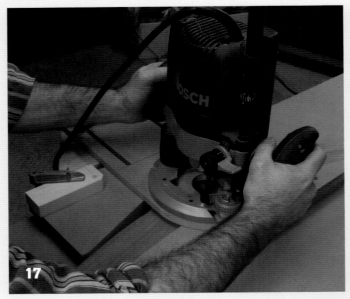

STEP 17 Rout the mortises in the hoops with a ³/8" spiral upcut bit. Guide the router along the straight edge with an edge guide. You can use a commercial guide, although it is quite easy to make one (plans are on page 36). Clamp stops to the top of the V to control the length of the mortises.

STEP 18 The V-block will align each hoop for four of the six mortises. The two mortises at the ends will prove more difficult as the hoop will only be in contact with one corner of the V. To accommodate this problem, trace the hoop onto the MDF surface when you have it clamped up for one of the interior mortises. Then align the hoop with the traced line when it comes time to rout the end mortises.

STEP 19 Chamfer the inside edge of the hoop and shape the outside edges with a ¹/4" roundover bit.

STEP 20 Cut the spreaders to size. Mortise both ends with the same ³/8" spiral upcut bit you used for the mortises in the hoops. Be sure to keep the same face against the jig when you cut each mortise. (Note: The shop-made edge guide works very well with the mortising jig.)

STEP 21 Round over all edges of the interior spreaders and the top edges of the end spreaders with a ¹/4" roundover bit. Bevel the bottom edges of the end spreaders to match the angles on the ends of the hoops.

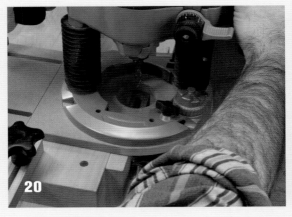

22

23

24

STEP 22 The glass shelves fit in dadoes routed across the inside faces of the hoops. Cut these dadoes with the help of a long straightedge. To get the straightedge set up in the right place, screw a length of 1×3 to the reference edge of the MDF. Butt the hoop up to the 1×3 and clamp it in place. Make three pairs of spacers — one pair for each shelf. The exact length of the spacers will depend on the width of your straight edge. Mark the shelf locations on one leg of the hoop and cut the spacers to position the straightedge accordingly. Use the spacers to locate the straightedge as you clamp it in position.

STEP 23 Rout the dados with a ³/₈" spiral upcut bit. With the router between you and the guiding fence on the straightedge, make the cuts from left to right. Use the other spacer pairs to locate the other sets of dadoes. Then use the same spacers to cut the dadoes on the second hoop.

STEP 24 Make up tenons for the joints as you did earlier. Glue the spreaders between the two hoops. I found it easier to clamp things up with the assembly on its side. After tightening the clamps, however, I stood it up so it could sit flat on its ends as the glue dried. When you are ready to put the entire unit together, center the hoop assembly on the drawer case and screw it in place with roundhead screws. I left these exposed so I could disassemble the piece to make it easier to move.

MAKING THE DRAWERS

STEP 1 Cut the pieces for the drawer boxes to size. Cut the corner joinery with a dovetail jig. I used the Leigh Jig, but any of those on the market will work as well. As there are so many different jigs available, I won't go into detail about how they work here. Consult your owner's manual for specifics about your particular model.

STEP 2 Rout a groove for the bottom in the drawer sides and fronts with a 1/4" straight bit in your table-mounted router. The top of the groove should align with the bottom edge of the drawer backs.

STEP 3 Glue the drawer boxes together, making sure to keep them square. After the glue dries, cut the drawer bottoms to fit and slide them in their grooves. Screw them to undersides of the drawer backs to fasten them in place.

STEP 4 Scrape, plane and sand the outsides of the drawers to fit them to their openings. Once you are satisfied with the fit, rout a shallow cove around each drawer front with a 3/8" cove bit. A small trim router works well for this operation.

STEP 5 Locate and glue drawer stops in the center of each drawer opening. Finish the unit with several coats of your favorite wood finish. I used Waterlox, a wiping varnish, on all of the exterior surfaces and shellac on the interiors of the drawers. I prefer to finish drawers with shellac as it leaves a much nicer residual odor than the other finishes. Finally, install the drawer pulls on the drawer fronts.

3

4

5

suppliers

**ADAMS & KENNEDY –
THE WOOD SOURCE**
6178 Mitch Owen Rd.
P.O. Box 700
Manotick, ON
Canada K4M 1A6
613-822-6800
www.wood-source.com
Wood supply

ADJUSTABLE CLAMP COMPANY
404 N. Armour St.
Chicago, IL 60622
312-666-0640
www.adjustableclamp.com
Clamps and woodworking tools

B&Q
Portswood House
1 Hampshire Corporate Park
Chandlers Ford
Eastleigh
Hampshire, England SO53 3YX
0845 609 6688
www.diy.com
*Woodworking tools, supplies and
hardware*

BUSY BEE TOOLS
130 Great Gulf Dr.
Concord, ON
Canada L4K 5W1
1-800-461-2879
www.busybeetools.com
Woodworking tools and supplies

**CONSTANTINE'S WOOD CENTER
OF FLORIDA**
1040 E. Oakland Park Blvd.
Fort Lauderdale, FL 33334
800-443-9667
www.constantines.com
Tools, woods, veneers, hardware

EAGLE AMERICA
Eagle America Corporation
510 Center Street
P.O. Box 1099
Chardon, OH 44024
800-872-2511
http://www.eagleamerica.com
*Router bits, workshop supplies and
finishing products*

**FRANK PAXTON LUMBER
COMPANY**
5701 W. 66th St.
Chicago, IL 60638
800-323-2203
www.paxtonwood.com
Wood, hardware, tools, books

JESSEM TOOL COMPANY
124 Big Bay Point Road
Barrie, Ontario
L4N 9B4
Canada
866-272-7492
www.jessem.com
Router tables and lifts

KLINGSPOR ABRASIVES INC.
2555 Tate Blvd. SE
Hickory, N.C. 28602
800-645-5555
www.klingspor.com
Sandpaper of all kinds

LEE VALLEY TOOLS LTD.
P.O. Box 1780
Ogdensburg, NY 13669-6780
800-871-8158 (U.S.)
800-267-8767 (Canada)
www.leevalley.com
Woodworking tools and hardware

LOWE'S COMPANIES, INC.
P.O. Box 1111
North Wilkesboro, NC 28656
800-445-6937
www.lowes.com
*Woodworking tools, supplies and
hardware*

PRICE CUTTER.COM
P.O. Box 1100
Chardon, OH 44024
888-288-2487
Router bits and accessories

**ROCKLER WOODWORKING AND
HARDWARE**
4365 Willow Dr.
Medina, MN 55340
800-279-4441
www.rockler.com
*Woodworking tools, hardware and
books*

TOOL TREND LTD.
140 Snow Blvd. Unit 1
Concord, ON
Canada L4K 4C1
416-663-8665
Woodworking tools and hardware

**TREND MACHINERY & CUTTING
TOOLS LTD.**
Odhams Trading Estate
St. Albans Rd.
Watford
Hertfordshire, U.K.
WD24 7TR
01923 224657
www.trendmachinery.co.uk
Woodworking tools and hardware

WINDY RIDGE WOODWORKS
6751 Hollenbach Road
New Tripoli, PA 18066
610-767-4515
www.wrwoodworks.com
*Fine furniture and woodworking
instruction*

WATERLOX COATINGS
908 Meech Ave.
Cleveland, OH 44105
800-321-0377
www.waterlox.com
Finishing supplies

WOODCRAFT SUPPLY LLC
1177 Rosemar Rd.
P.O. Box 1686
Parkersburg, WV 26102
800-535-4482
www.woodcraft.com
Woodworking hardware

WOODWORKER'S HARDWARE
P.O. Box 180
Sauk Rapids, MN 56379-0180
800-383-0130
www.wwhardware.com
Woodworking hardware

WOODWORKER'S SUPPLY
1108 N. Glenn Rd.
Casper, WY 82601
800-645-9292
http://woodworker.com
*Woodworking tools and accessories,
finishing supplies, books and plans*

index

MORE GREAT TITLES FROM POPULAR WOODWORKING!

CUTTING-EDGE BAND SAW TIPS & TRICKS

By Ken Burton

It's time to unleash the full power of your band saw. In this book you'll learn how to build jigs and fixtures that will turn your band was into the most useful tool in your shop. There are also three projects that show you how to your new jigs and fixtures and harness the power of your band saw.

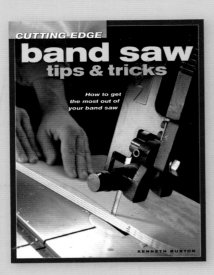

ISBN 13: 978-1-55870-702-3
ISBN 10: 1-55870-702-6
paperback, 128 p., #70653

BOX BY BOX

By Jim Stack

Hone your woodworking skills one box at a time. In the pages of this book you'll find plans for 21 delightful boxes along with step-by-step instructions for making them. the projects include basic boxes that a novice can make with just a few hand tools to projects that will provide experienced woodworkers with an exciting challenge.

ISBN 13: 978-1-55870-774-0
ISBN 10: 1-55870-774-3
hardcover w/concealed wire-o, 144 p., # 70725

TABLE SAW PROJECTS WITH KEN BURTON

By Ken Burton

The table saw is the most versatile power tool in your woodworking shop. Short of applying the final finish, the table saw can do tricks you never thought possible. As a bonus, this book comes with a DVD of the author giving you live demonstrations of the techniques he talks about in his book as well as how to use the table saw safely.

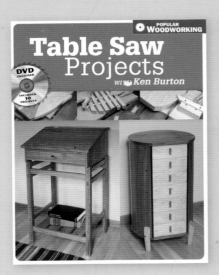

ISBN 13: 978-1-55870-778-8
ISBN 10: 1-55870-778-6
paperback w/DVD, 128 p., #Z0030

WOODSHOP STORAGE SOLUTIONS

By Ralph Laughton

Are you constantly looking for better and more efficient ways of storing and using your tools? this book contains 16 ingenious projects that will make your woodshop totally efficient, extremely flexible and very safe. Projects include: down-draft table, clamp rack, mobile table saw stand, router trolley, router table and more.

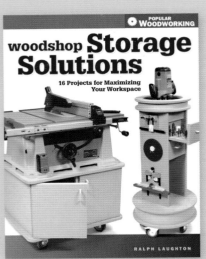

ISBN 13: 978-1-55870-784-9
ISBN 10: 1-55870-784-0
paperback, 128 p., # Z0348

These and other great woodworking books are available at your local bookstore, woodworking stores or from online suppliers.

www.popularwoodworking.com